Albert The Chicken Man

Albert Okura

JUAN POLLO

*This book is dedicated to all those I may
have offended and pushed to the limit in
my quest to serve perfect chicken to every
customer.   Albert Okura.*

Albert The Chicken Man

Albert The Chicken Man

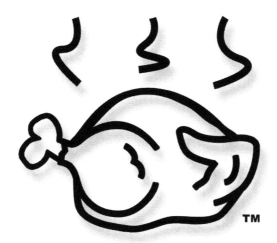

JUAN POLLO ™

The Best Tasting Chicken!

EST. 1984

ALBERT OKURA
THE CHICKEN MAN ™

With a 50 year plan

SECOND EDITION

ABOUT THIS BOOK

This book will appeal to two different types of readers:

1. Fans of Juan Pollo chicken who are interested in the history of their favorite chicken restaurant and potential investment opportunities.

2. Individuals who are intrigued by success stories of others and how it may apply to their life experiences.

I intended to follow the traditional path of writing a self-congratulatory autobiography. That includes starting at the bottom, learning and making mistakes along the way, toiling in the chains, starting my own restaurant, turning it into a world wide chain, retiring a wealthy man, then writing my memoirs.

Carlos Garcia Aceves, a friend and publisher, pointed out that my theory was incorrect – there is a new world wide internet generation hungry for success stories of small businesses like Juan Pollo and they are interested in the present, not the far off future or the long ago past. The right people who can help the company will have the opportunity to find out about us.

In my youth, I would go to bookstores and purchase autobiographies of successful business entrepreneurs such as Ray Kroc, owner of McDonalds, and Sam Walton, founder of Wal-Mart. I would devour these types of books to try and analyze why they succeeded and others failed.

Reading these books was inspirational but all the people I read about were either retired or deceased. I did not have the opportunity to work for these men while they were on their way up.

Albert The Chicken Man

Published by
LCM PUBLISHING
PO BOX 1257
Fontana, CA 92335
www.albertthechickenman.com
www.Juanpollo.com

LCM ISBN 978-0-9834169-1-3
E-Pub ISBN 978-0-9834171-1-3
Third Edition Printed in the United States of America

This book is registered with the Writters Guild of the West
For more info go to WGA.org
Registered with the USA Library of Congress
NO 487686983565365837.

If you would like to send comments send them to:
albertokura@juanpollo.com

FANS of Juan Pollo will enjoy this book, - Zoe

Albert The Chicken Man

Table Of Contents

Albert The Chicken Man

"SAN PEDRO SKIPPERS" 1939

MY NAME IS 'TEE' OKURA. I WAS A STAR BASEBALL PLAYER WHEN I WAS YOUNG BUT I NEVER WENT INTO BUSINESS LIKE MY SON ALBERT. THIS IS HIS STORY ....

1

INTRODUCTION

From the time I can remember, I believed I would accomplish something great in my life. It took me over 30 years to understand what that destiny was.

Entering high school in 1967, I knew it was time to start planning my future. I didn't know where to start. Counselors, teachers, parents, family members stressed the importance of college education but in those days everyone's advice seemed to be the same: doctor, lawyer, scientist, teacher, architect, etc. The more I thought about things the more confused I became. Because I was Asian/American, everyone assumed I was college material.

I wasn't smart enough to be a lawyer or scientist, much less a doctor or dentist (my mother's personal favorite). Had someone told me to be an entrepreneur, I would have perked up quick.

1970 - while attending Los Angeles Jr. College I stumbled into a minimum wage, $1.15/hour job at Burger King cooking hamburgers. Even though my weekly checks were seldom over $30 a week I became hooked on the fast food environment.

By the age of 20, I quit school and jumped into the fast food business. In 1984, I opened my own fast food restaurant selling rotisserie chicken.

I was in the right place at the right time and I took advantage. My destiny in life is to sell more chicken than anyone in the world. I have been picking up valuable life lessons that will help me fulfill my destiny. I am moving as fast as I have people in place.

-ALBERT OKURA, JUAN POLLO FOUNDER

GINA

2

CHILDHOOD IN THE 50s

My grandparents left Japan in the early 1910s to seek a better life in America. Typical of the early Japanese immigrants, they settled in Southern California and became farmers.

My father, Tsuyoshi, nicknamed 'Tee', was born in 1916, the second oldest of eight children. My mother, Chiyoko, nicknamed 'Chickie', was born in 1923 and was the second oldest of seven children.

My parents' generation experienced tremendous challenges while growing up. In the 1920s they had to learn English in school and go home to a traditional Japanese environment. The 1930s brought the Great Depression which forced all family members to find work where they could in order to make ends meet.

My father was a natural athlete. Although short in stature, he was blessed with a bodybuilder's physique and excelled in almost every sport he tried. As a youth, he became very proficient in judo. It taught him body control and the value of using leverage. In high school he did shot put, pole vault, high hurdles, sprints and long jump. He was the captain of his basketball teams and star of his

Tsuyoshi & Chiyoko Okura (1948)

baseball teams. The biggest sport in the Japanese community was baseball. The whole community would show up every Sunday to watch the Japanese baseball leagues. My father played for the San Pedro Skippers. He pitched, played center field, and batted cleanup. He was the star player on the best team. The Japanese-American newspaper *Rafu Shimpo* would later call my dad the greatest all around Japanese-American athlete of his generation. I believe my father was a great athlete because he refused to lose and would do what ever it took to win.

World War II brought upheaval to the Japanese-American families who lived along the coast in Southern California. They were ordered to detention camps where they stayed for most of the war.

My father was in the United States Army when detention was ordered. He was stationed in Texas but never saw action overseas. His younger brother, Susumu, volunteered for combat duty in the 442nd infantry unit comprised solely of Japanese-American soldiers. He passed away in Italy fighting the Germans.

After the war, my parents married and settled in Wilmington, California, which is also known as the Port of Los Angeles.

I was born Albert Ryo Okura, in 1951, the second oldest of four children. I inherited my father's drive and attitude but not his athletic body or skills. This would lead to early frustration until I learned how to channel my energy to business. I am a 'Baby Boomer', part of the largest group of American-born babies in our nation's history, past or present. 'The Boomers', a product of the World War II generation, reaped the benefits of their hard work.

The 50s was a great time to grow up. Unscathed by the war America became the most powerful industrial and economic force in the world. There was a strong work ethic, relatively low crime rate, emphasis on education, and a strong sense of patriotism. The communist threat was not yet in full bloom.

When I was five years old I was nervous about attending kindergarten and didn't want to go. By first grade, I made friends but was shy in the classroom. I was very active and excelled in outdoor playground activities such as kick ball, basketball, and softball. After school, the playground would stay open until 5:00 p.m. so I would play until closing and then walk home. During the summer months we would play touch football and baseball in the alley behind our house until it was too dark to see. My mother would yell out the kitchen window for us to come and eat dinner.

Life was much simpler in the 50s. Our family had one telephone, one black and white television, two radios, and two cars. I remember the joy I had when the Japanese invented an affordable battery operated transistor radio that allowed us to listen to Dodger baseball and Laker basketball games anywhere. Our black and white T.V. was challenging because in those days there were many tubes inside the console that always seemed to burn out. Someone had to pull them out, take them to the nearest market and see if they had a replacement. Once the T.V. was working, we had to re-adjust the antennae every time we changed the channel.

Speaking of channels, there were only seven available in the 50s and of course there were no color shows. In those early years almost everything we learned came from the classrooms because there was no such invention as a computer and its companion, the

Albert & older brother Robert Okura (1958)

Internet. From Kindergarten to 12th grade the classroom hours were 8 a.m. to 3 p.m. There were few holiday days off. Sometimes I felt like I was a prisoner. The thing I looked forward to every year was the 12 weeks of summer vacation. Every year my mother arranged for us to go to Yosemite and camp out for at least one week. These vacations provided some of my favorite childhood memories.

Life Lesson Learned:
Looking back in time always makes you wonder how you survived and found a way to enjoy life without modern conveniences.

Yosemite vacation with sisters Amy, Susan and Mom. (1960)

3

YOUTH AND FAST FOOD HEAVEN

1960 - My mother decided that it was time for me to get a job because she wanted to teach me responsibility. She took me to the *San Pedro News-Pilot* and signed me up to deliver papers after school. I didn't really have a choice but I thought it would be a good experience.

The good news was my parents bought me a new thirty dollar bicycle and that gave me freedom to go just about anywhere I wanted but the bad news was I only made thirty dollars a month so I had to budget money carefully. I could spend one dollar a day. I supplemented the one dollar a day by picking up empty Coca Cola bottles and redeeming them for three cents at grocery stores. Most of my money went to comic books, baseball cards, Coca Cola and hamburgers.

I knew the best places to buy hamburgers. With my new bicycle, I was very mobile and riding two or three miles for a hamburger was not out of the question. The cheapest hamburger in town was twenty-nine cents.

1962 - Albert wins paperboy award of excellence. *San Pedro News Pilot.*

1961- McDonald's hamburgers opened across town. Their specialty was fifteen cent hamburgers and ten cent French fries. Everyone in town was amazed at their low prices. From the day they opened, there were lines of customers. They were so busy that their food was always fresh. Our Sunday night treat was getting everyone in the car and going to McDonald's for dinner. I didn't know it at the time, but besides my enjoying their food and low price, McDonald's would have a huge affect on my life.

The 1960s was the golden age of fast food chains. New chains exploded on the scene and each one of them was inspired by the success of McDonald's.

Taco Bell established as a Mexican fast food restaurant chain selling fifteen cent hard shell tacos and fifteen cent bean burritos. A & W Root Beer sold five cent ice-cold mugs of their root beer.

Early 1960s McDonald's Restaurant.

Der Wienersnitzel sold three different fifteen cent hotdogs. Kentucky Fried Chicken sold fried chicken by the bucket. Jack in the box sold eighteen cent hamburgers and was open twenty-four a day. In-N-Out Burgers sold burgers and fries that were sold through a double drive thru. Foster's Freeze sold malts, shakes, rootbeer floats, ice cream cones, banana splits and almost any type of ice cream. I loved all these new restaurants. What a great time for someone like me.

Life lesson learned:
In the 1960s, fast food burst upon the scene, made many people wealthy, and most importantly, made a lot of kids happy.

12 year old 7th grade hamburger expert. (1963)

4

TWO BOOKS THAT CHANGED MY LIFE.

Like most families, my mother had a big influence in my life. She made me deliver newspapers at an early age, she encouraged me to play little league baseball and basketball, she took me to the public swimming pools so I would learn how to swim, she taught me responsibility by making me wash and iron my own clothes, she encouraged me to be able to cook for myself, and she made sure I was doing well in school.

She gave me two books that changed my life:

1. *How to Win Friends and Influence People*, by Dale Carnegie.

2. *Think and Grow Rich* by Napoleon Hill.

Dale Carnegie spent his life observing and studying people and their ability to get along in groups and individually. He studied the greatest salesmen in the world to learn their secrets of persuasion. He wrote everything he learned in his book *How to Win Friends and Influence People*.

Each chapter talked about such topics as turning enemies into friends, getting strangers to become friends, or persuading others to your way of thinking.

The most inspirational books I have read.

Dale Carnegie found that the secret is to take a sincere interest in the other person, talk about their wants and desires before yours, and find areas in which you can offer genuine compliments. You will have few arguments if you find room for agreement.

Think and Grow Rich had an even greater affect on my thinking. Napoleon Hill studied the most successful businesspersons of the early 20th century. He wanted to find out why some people rose to greatness and others failed. He discovered the universal traits that every self-made successful man possesses. These billionaires instinctively possessed these traits and made their fortunes without reading self-help books.

Napoleon Hill became wealthy by studying, dissecting and analyzing the habits of the truly rich. He put this in book form with thirteen principles for success. When I first read Think and Grow Rich, I didn't think I could apply what I read into real life. I kept

Albert getting advice from his mother. Wilmington, California (1965)

reading this book over and over to get inspired but because I didn't have specific goals it was hard to focus attention on accomplishing something.

The essence of the book is that you need to decide what your goal is, pursue it and let nothing stop you from achieving success. By the time I reached my thirties I understood how to apply the principles of both books in my life. I believe every self-made man knowingly or instinctively understands the principals of these two books.

Life Lesson Learned:
The secret of life is understanding the power of your brain and what it could do for you.

Albert The Chicken Man

Albert at age 17 with his 1955 Chevrolet. (1968) High School Senior.

5

COMPULSIVE BEHAVIOR CAN BE A GOOD THING

I discovered early in life that I could be very compulsive. Whenever I did things that interested me I would become consumed by it.

At ten years old I became a fan of the New York Yankees so I started to collect Yankee baseball cards. I would spend every last cent I had on packages of cards. I wasn't content with one or two cards of each player; I wanted twenty or thirty. For example, I had over forty mint condition 1961 Mickey Mantle cards that were later worth much money. Eventually they were all stolen.

After that I started to buy Marvel comic books. They were only twelve cents so it was easy to start collecting. Some stores sold old issues. at a discount so I would bicycle for miles to search for issues. I ended up with hundreds of books. These were also stolen and I have nothing to show for my comic book days.

I got hooked on building plastic model cars. It was popular to buy these kits that you had to assemble yourself. I am not even sure why I took up this hobby because I ended up with model cars

Albert spent hours building plastic model cars similar to this one.

everywhere. There is no practical purpose to owning fragile plastic model cars.

Along the way, I became addicted to television. There were fewer than ten different channels but I would watch hour after hour regardless of what was on. The only good thing about this habit was that it was free.

After high school, I decided to try smoking. Within six months, I became a chain smoker smoking over two packs of cigarettes a day (I quit cold turkey when I was twenty-nine years old.)

While attending junior college I took ceramics classes making pop art sculptures. My ceramics teacher didn't appreciate me because I worked on mass-producing large sculptures and they took up too much room in the oven. I would spend entire days working on ceramics projects. When I dropped out of college I quit ceramics and never looked back.

When I went into Burger King Management, my compulsive behavior started to work in my favor. I spent hour after hour of

Albert became obsessed with making large ceramic sculptures while in Jr. College. (1970)

unpaid extra work learning the trade. Being a workaholic is a good trait if you want to open your own business.

After Juan Pollo opened I spent every waking minute learning how to cook perfect chickens and how to beat the competition. I was relentless in my pursuit to make it successful.

Life Lesson Learned:
Obsessive-compulsive behavior can be a valuable trait if applied in a productive way.

More of Albert's sculptures. (1970)

6

PATTON'S DESTINY

During high school years I was trying to find my way. There was pressure to declare what you would do after high school. Most of my teachers and counselors had good intentions and were good people, but I wasn't inspired by any advice they offered. I did O.K. in the classrooms but I was just going through the motions.

Graduating high school in 1969 and not sure what to major in or what college to attend, I enrolled at the local Jr. College. That first semester, my history teacher mentioned to the class that 'Patton' was the best movie he had ever seen. The Academy Awards gave 'Patton' the Oscar for best picture in 1970.

I didn't know much about World War II except from watching war movies with John Wayne defeating either the Germans or Japanese. I went to see a war movie about General George Patton instead I saw a movie about a man so driven by his perceived destiny in life that he let nothing stop him from accomplishing his goals.

General George Smith Patton Jr. (1942)

He believed his destiny was to lead his troops to victory in the greatest and most glorious war the world had ever seen. He recognized this at an early age, prepared himself by studying every major battle in recorded history and pursued a course of action that put him in position before and during the war to fulfill his destiny. General Patton believed he was the reincarnation of the greatest generals in history. Known as 'Old Blood and Guts', General Patton commanded the third army and became the most feared American military commander.

General George Smith Patton Jr. (1942)   2014 Corbis Images

It is said that General Patton's troops advanced further, captured more enemy prisoners and liberated more territories in less time than any army in military history.

It can be debated whether General Patton was misguided in his beliefs, but the end result is that he fulfilled his destiny. Patton passed away shortly after the war due to a freak car accident. I realized that if you work your whole life to accomplish something great and then you achieve it, your purpose in life may be over.

Life Lesson Learned:
If you have a destiny in life, you will realize it and work relentlessly to fulfill that destiny.

1971 - Joining the Van Club craze of the 70s Albert drove his custom 1965 Chevrolet Van to Burger King everyday many times sleeping inside over night so he would not be late to work.

7

BURGER KING - A WILD RIDE

1970 - I was attending Los Angeles Junior College and realized I didn't have money for gas or other expenses. I went to the job placement department at the college and looked for part time work. The job position that interested me the most was Burger King.

I didn't know it at the time but Florida based Burger King was the second largest hamburger chain in America. The college made an appointment for a job interview. Mike Edwards the Restaurant Supervisor at the Harbor City location interviewed me and hired me for part time work at a pay rate of one dollar and fifteen cents per hour. I ate my first quarter pound Whopper that day and thought it was delicious.

I was happy making thirty to forty dollars a week because that was much better than the thirty dollars a month I used to make delivering newspapers. This Burger King wasn't too busy so it was easy to learn the various jobs. Burger King had an organized and structured system. Each employee had a primary job and a secondary job. There also was a position hierarchy. The manager's responsibility was to 'expedite' or assemble the customer's orders and hand

Burger King's original Double Whopper Sandwhich.

them out. The next best employee assembled the hamburgers on the front line then the order taker/cashier. The remaining four positions were broiler man, fry man, drink person, and dining room host.

I realized if I mastered each position and became the best worker I would never have to worry about job security. Mike kept asking me to go into management but the idea never interested me. Eventually Mike was terminated for unexplained reasons and was replaced by Bill Johnston.

I was impressed by Bill's enthusiasm for the job and his work ethic. In a short time I became Bill's right hand man. He also encouraged me to go into management. I still had little interest and turned him down. In the meantime my stay at Jr. College was ending. I attended college so I wouldn't be drafted into the Vietnam War. When President Nixon stopped the draft in 1971, I quit going to school.

I was twenty-one years old and realized I better start learning a profession. Almost all of my high school friends were attending college and working on their diplomas. I decided to become a Burger King Supervisor. Bill was happy with my decision and immediately took me under his wing. Starting as an Assistant Manager #2, I had to work nights and swing shifts. Since I was a night person, this worked out perfect for me. After I got settled into a routine, Bill sat me down and told me the secret to getting promotions.

First I needed to master all the duties of the Manager #2. Then, on my own time I needed to learn and perform the duties of the Assistant Manager #1. If you worked like, and acted like a Manager #1 they would have to promote you. Using this strategy I moved up the ranks quickly. Within a year I received my promotion to Store Supervisor. Even though I spent many unpaid hours learning the next positions I approached it as a hobby and I enjoyed every minute. My promotion was to a store in a high crime area that experienced high management turnover. As a young ambitious first time Supervisor I had high hopes of being the ultimate problem solver and 'saving' the location. I was in for a culture shock. I wasn't used to working in an area where anyone or everyone might rob you.

After one year I was working longer hours and getting less done. The store was beating me down mentally and physically. My District Manager recognized that I was burned out and transferred me to a different store before I got too frustrated and resigned. There were three things that I learned from my experience in Inglewood. The first is if you set personal goals that are easily met you will lose focus because there nothing left to accomplish except mentally burning out. The second is that idealism doesn't work in business. One person cannot change the world or make people change their ways. To survive bad situations, you have to do the best you can with what you've got. The third is that no matter what your personal work habits are you need to pace yourself to avoid burning out physically.

I was transferred to the Burger King in Carson, California. The difference in the two stores was like day and night. I had time to sit back and analyze what had happened and vowed to never let mental breakdown slow me down again.

Soon I was flourishing at this Burger King. There was an assembly line system in place that was able to handle a line of customers within minutes. When operating at full speed we were able to serve one customer every twenty-seconds. Many times customers would receive their order seconds after they received their change. I was learning about sales volume and the value of mass production.

There were nine employees on the assembly line and each had a specific function. First was the order taker who wrote up the orders. The ticket was handed to the cashier who collected the money. On the food assembly line one person operated the conveyor belt broiler that automatically cooked the hamburger patties and buns.

From there the Whoppers and Cheese Whoppers were assembled by a person on the front of the assembly line and the Jr. Whoppers and regular hamburgers assembled on the back side. The next person cooked the French fries. He was in charge of keeping up with the French fries during the rushes and cooking the onion rings and fish filets when ordered.

The last person on the production line was the drink person who was in charge of the soft drinks and the shakes. As the manager, I was the 'Expeditor,' or person who directed and positioned the employees, bagged up each customers order, double checked accuracy and handed orders out to correct customer.

The final employee was the dining room host who kept everything clean. The Supervisor I replaced assembled the majority of the employees and I was able to fine tune the operations. Our crew put on a show for customers with fast delivery and accuracy of orders. It was common for orders to be filled by the time customers received their change. What I learned from this experience was the value of teamwork and positioning of employees to best fit their skills. Working at the Carson location revitalized me. At the same

BurgerKing has grown to be the world's second largest hamburger chain.

time there were huge changes in the fast food industry.

The first major change was the computer age. During the early 1970s inventory control was accomplished with an old fashioned mechanical adding machine. Figuring food cost percentages relied on long division because calculators were not available. Inventory control was slow and cumbersome. As new technology was introduced, Burger King was quick to adopt anything that improved cash or inventory controls. They knew this was vital for a company to continue to expand.

I remember how amazed I was when the company introduced new ten thousand dollar cash registers that transmitted daily sales information and inventory every night through the telephone lines.

The early 1970s was a time of desegregation and quota systems in America. By the time I entered the management ranks of Burger King I was the only non-anglo manager in the meetings. Companies were mandated by the federal government to have a certain percentage of minority managers. I always considered myself a normal American but now I am considered a minority. I have learned to go with the flow. I can tell people I'm a minority when it is convenient and I can tell others I am a red-blooded American when it is convenient.

The fast food companies were racing to open as many locations as possible. Burger King owned by the deep pockets of Pillsbury Foods was competing with McDonald's to become the largest chain in America. Burger King began franchising and this created a buying frenzy for locations. Areas and territories were being snapped up left and right. Corporate executives were jumping ship to buy a franchise.

By the mid 1970s these franchises were opening nationwide. In those hectic early days the entire town would show up for a grand opening. Burger King's corporate office sent one supervisor and one district manager to each grand opening. It was exhausting work because each new store had to hire at least one hundred new employees and train them in less than one week. When the stores opened for business there were lines of customers from 11am until 8pm everyday. There were fifty employees working each shift and usually no one knew what to do. Corporate staffing who attended these openings came back looking like zombies and complained how hard they had to work.

I attended the Redding, Simi Valley, and San Bernardino grand openings. Recalling my early experience of burning out I decided to mentally prepare myself to be the first one to be at work, be the last one to leave and never act tired or complain. I learned to pace myself, not to panic, and stay calm in the face of hundreds of customers. My philosophy was, 'Do the best you can with what you've got.'

With the company expanding so fast and so many executives resigning to become franchisees there were tremendous opportunities available for anyone with ambition. I never set personal goals beyond becoming a unit supervisor so I wasn't sure what I should do. I was too young to be a franchisee and I was concerned if I moved up

Albert holding his collectable doll from his Burger King days in the 1970s (2012)

the corporate ladder, I would be transferred to another part of the country.

I always wondered why Burger King did not use their chain driven broilers to cook Whoppers to order instead of using steam tables and microwave ovens. Somehow the idea of a microwave hamburger as your signature product doesn't seem right.

Burger King has grown to be the second largest hamburger chain in the world, but in all the years I worked there, no one ever said 'That's the best hamburger I ever ate!' In the back of my mind I didn't want to be fifty years old and tell people that I worked for Burger King.

I knew it was time to leave.

Life Lesson Learned:
If destiny awaits you, you must to be willing to give up security.

1977 - Ray Millman planted the seed in Albert's head about purchasing and owning an entire town.

8

RAY MILLMAN - "I COULD HAVE OWNED A TOWN"

During my high school years I read every book I could about investing in real estate but I never learned how to apply this knowledge in real life.

The mid 1970s was a period of high inflation. The dollar lost its buying power and gasoline prices doubled almost overnight. To keep up with inflation many turned to investing in real estate. Houses in Southern California were doubling in value every couple of years. It was a crazy time and I witnessed many people making piles of money buying and selling real estate. I watched this whole phenomenon happening right in front of me while I sat by on the sidelines.

1977 - I met Ray Millman while working at Burger King in Torrance, California. Ray was a regular customer who sold real estate. When I mentioned my interest in real estate Ray jumped at the chance to sell me my first property. He immediately showed me a two-bedroom house for $69,000 and arranged all the paperwork so all I had to do was sign on the dotted line. I was happy to get my feet wet in a real estate investment even though I could have bought the same house two years earlier for about $30,000.

3134 187th Pl Torrance   11-15-78

First real estate investment. Torrance, California (1978)

I owned the house for one year and made every mistake an inexperienced landlord could make, such as renting to friends, letting them destroy the house, and letting them pay no rent before being evicted. I was frustrated but managed to sell the house for $77,000 which covered all the expenses and losses. I used this as a learning experience.

I got to know Ray as a friend. One day he told me a story about a lost opportunity to own a town. After World War II, land in California was plentiful and inexpensive. Ray told me that he should have bought acreage and built his own town. It would have been so easy in those days. He could have been mayor or police chief or whatever he desired. He regretted that he never took action and I never forgot Ray's story about owning a town. Twenty-five years later I was confronted with a similar situation but unlike Ray I jumped at an opportunity to own my own town.

Life lesson Learned:

You snooze, you lose. If opportunity presents itself, you need to take action.

9

JOHNNY JOHNSON – 'THE GREATEST BUSINESSPERSON'

1977- It was a boom time for most fast food chains especially Burger King. Fast food chains discovered the advantages of growing quickly through franchising. They were expanding so fast that they couldn't keep up with staffing at the corporate offices.

That year I met Mr. Johnny Johnson owner of Azusa Greens Country Club. He called out of the blue and offered me a job as his golf course general manager even though I had never golfed before.

I went to Azusa for an interview. Mr. Johnson was a self-made multimillionaire who knew how to make money and once told me that everything he touched turned to gold. Although I had never golfed I fit Mr. Johnson's profile for his general manager because he needed someone without 'baggage' that he could mold to his rules at his golf course.

When I first met Mr. Johnson he told me he liked the way I moved. I didn't know what he meant. He told me that he could analyze a person's traits by the way they walked across the room. It's a good thing that I always walk at a brisk confident pace or he might not have hired me.

Albert The Chicken Man

Azusa Greens Country Club located in the foothills of San Gabriel Mountains (1979)

One of Mr. Johnson's selling points was to tell me that as a supervisor of Burger King, I would be one manager out of thousands of fast food managers. As the general manager at his golf course, I would be in exclusive company because there were only so many golf courses.

I knew I had to work for Mr. Johnson because he possessed a certain mental toughness and attitude that I needed to learn. The first thing Mr. Johnson taught me was the three most important rules of his business or any business: 1 Simplify. 2 Simplify. 3 Simplify.

He told me the biggest mistake companies make is having too much rules and regulations. Mr. Johnson insisted on simplicity.

Mr. Johnson taught me to break down everything into its simplest form. When placing ads for the golf course Mr. Johnson would analyze every word to end up with the least amount of words that conveyed the most powerful meaning.

I learned that Mr. Johnson made his first million dollars before the age of twenty. He told me that he followed real estate appraisers and talked to owners who had their property appraised. He would offer to buy their property for one half of the appraised value. I asked him why anyone would sell at a low price. He said, "You would be surprised." I realized Mr. Johnson instinctively knew every persuasive principle used by Dale Carnegie in his book *How to Win Friends and Influence People.*

Mr. Johnson made his second fortune getting into the asphalt paving business. After World War II, developers were building hundreds of tract houses in every town in Southern California and Mr. Johnson realized that every new house needed an asphalt driveway. He soon became one of the largest asphalt companies in the state by making deals with the builders.

In the 1970s Mr. Johnson bought five hundred acres of undeveloped land in the foothills of the San Gabriel Mountains. He probably paid less than five hundred dollars per acre. First he took one hundred twenty acres to build the golf course and then leased it out. Thanks to the new eighteen hole golf course the other vacant acreage gained much value.

Pot O' Gold Tournament Winner recieves check from General Manager Albert Okura (1979)

He then sold acres along the golf course to builders who then constructed houses. In time there were houses built on all the available land except for one acre directly in front of the golf course clubhouse. Mr. Johnson saved this for last because when he eventually sold it for $100,000 the value of his one hundred-twenty acre golf course was $12 million.

During one of his private lectures Mr. Johnson mentioned that many people claimed they were 'millionaires' but their wealth was based on equity and net worth not actual cash. Mr. Johnson said those who were truly wealthy have access to money. He mentioned that he kept one million dollars in the bank for his spending money.

After one year, I knew it was time to leave. Even though it was the most informative year I ever experienced. I was a poor general manager because I wasn't a natural salesman and I was a night person not the early bird needed to run a golf course.

I felt guilty that I was getting paid to learn the secrets of business from a millionaire instead of me paying him.

Life Lesson Learned:
The three most important ingredients in business are simplify, simplify, simplify.

10

'WANNABE' REAL ESTATE TYCOON

I knew that I couldn't learn anything else from Mr. Johnson. Like most ambitious young adults I had dreams to become a real estate tycoon. Unfortunately I lacked the two most important qualities to become a real tycoon: capital, and the ability to 'wheel and deal' with sellers as well as buyers.

My mother always encouraged me to learn how to invest. During the 1960s, my parents started buying low-income rental properties. They didn't have much capital so they bought the most they could for whatever they could save. My father was a handyman so he did all the maintenance on the properties.

My father was always busy working to support our family so I rationalized that it would be a good idea to spend some time working with him before I went out on my own. In reality it was a good idea for me to use his money since I didn't have any of my own.

My first step was to try to obtain a real estate license so I would have a better understanding of the nuts and bolts of the business. In those days the only requirement was to pass a one hundred-fifty question exam but I didn't want to read real estate law books and study for a test – I had phobias about anything that reminded me of high school or college.

Relocation crew moving the apartment during the midnight hours. (1980)

Finally I decided to go ahead and take the test no matter what. I took a real estate license seminar and they sold sample test questions with the answers. I bought all the sample test and memorized all the answers. I took the test and recognized every question from the samples. I knew I passed successfully.

During the 1970s condominiums became the easiest way for first time buyers to invest in real estate. Many apartment owners replaced their buildings with new condominiums. Whenever possible these apartment buildings were sold so they could be relocated.

My father owned a vacant property in Wilmington, California that was zoned to accept a move on apartment building. It was a cheaper alternative than building new. I found a five-unit apartment that needed to be moved and a mover that would move it for a total cost of fifty-thousand dollars. That sounded reasonable to me so I persuaded my father to sign the deal and we got into the apartment renovation business.

I spent the next year working on this project with my father. It proved a good learning process. I learned the basics of the construction business such as foundation work, electrical, plumbing, carpentry, drywall, painting, and roofing.

'Tee' removing the support beams that held the building while being transported.

After completing the apartments we refinanced the property and used the money to do another move-on apartment about two miles away. This time we moved a six-unit apartment building.

During my real estate construction career I learned a valuable lesson about applying knowledge learned in school and its practical application in real life. While attending junior college I took

classes in drafting and architecture to satisty graduation requirements. To me it was drawing accurate lines and being very detailed in measurements. I treated these classes as nothing more than schoolwork. By the time I started doing construction with my father

Albert working on the roof (1980)

we had to submit blueprints to the city. I realized I not only understood blueprints I also knew how to draw them. I had learned a valuable skill without even realizing it.

It was good that I spent two years working with my father but I knew I could never become the wealthiest real estate investor in the area so I knew it was time to move on.

Life Lesson Learned:
Real estate investing for the average person is difficult.

Finished apartment building (1980)

11

DEL TACO – TUNE-UP FOR SUCCESS

1981 - I decided that making a living investing in rental properties was not for me because dealing with tenants and their problems can be challenging. It was not something I wanted to do for the rest of my life. At age twenty-nine I knew it was time to get back into a 'real' work routine. At the same time I realized that the only profession I truly enjoyed was the fast food business so I started researching the various chains.

Burger King and McDonald's were so huge I would get lost in the shuffle. I remembered my mentor at Burger King, Tony Rolland, telling me that he was impressed with a small chain in San Bernardino County called Del Taco.

When I was young my two favorite restaurants were McDonald's and Taco Bell. Del Taco was a combination of both. They served hamburgers and French fries on one side of the kitchen and tacos and burritos on the other side.

The founder of Del Taco, Ed Hackbarth previously worked for the founder of Taco Bell, Glen Bell. Bell grew up eating at the original McDonald's in San Bernardino and was inspired by McDonald's fast food system. It seems I was destined to work at Del Taco.

Ed Hackbarth founder of Del Taco shows Albert picture of his first location in Yermo, Ca (2011)

1964 - Ed Hackbarth opened his first Del Taco in Yermo, California. Originally called Casa Del Taco, Ed shortened the name to Del Taco as he started opening additional restaurants in the area. Although Ed later sold the company, as of 2011 he still actively participates in operating about five of the higher volume Del Tacos. I respect the fact that the founder of the company still finds the time to help the stores. It sends a positive message throughout the company.

One of the qualities that set Del Taco apart from the competition was a sense of family. Burger King was cold hearted when it came to treating the management personel. When their managers had problems they were eliminated and never allowed to be rehired. On the other hand it was common for eliminated Del Taco managers to later be re-hired at different locations. No one was kicked out permanently because they made mistakes.

I applied for a managment position and interviewed at the

Del Taco Carson #67 wins company Christmas Decorating Contest. (1982)

Carson location. The District Manager, John Cyprus interviewed me and after a few questions and answers hired me on the spot. I was assigned for training at a location in Torrance, California. I was a manager trainee assigned to training supervisor Leona Perry. Although I had been out of the business for almost four years I acted like I knew everything about the business and told Leona I was ready to become supervisor. I didn't even bother to read the operating manual. The first Friday Leona thought she would teach me a lesson by leaving me in charge of the Friday night rush by myself. I was rusty and didn't have a good grasp for the workflow. The employees started running the show and things got out of hand. Soon there was a backlog of orders. There were angry customers everywhere. It was a mess. I knew I had much catching up to do. I spent the next few weeks learning each of the work positions and working on running the shifts.

Every time John would check up on me I told him I was ready to get promoted to supervisor. Two more weeks passed and John called to inform me he was eliminating the Unit Supervisor at the Carson location. The store failed its quality assurance audit for the second-straight time and Carson was the worst performing store in his district. John told me he was promoting me to supervisor and I should fire all the hourly employees.

I never met Doug, the previous supervisor, and when they told me he was only eighteen years old I felt sorry for him because I knew that he was just a teenager who was in over his head.

I never finished reading the operating manual so I didn't know how to prepare some of the basic food items such as the re-fried beans and the hamburger meat for the tacos. I spent much time after closing time getting up to speed with the cooking procedures. I knew that the crew was apprehensive about me being their new supervisor and they were demoralized after volunteering many hours in two failed attempts to pass audits. I didn't put the crew down and didn't complain about their lack of help. I started repairing broken equipment and reorganized the store.

The re-inspection was scheduled in one month. I studied the previous failed inspections and found most of the violations were due to lack of cleanliness, broken equipment, or improper food handling. Lack of experienced management and leadership were the main culprits. I was very experienced with preparing for quality assurance audits so I wasn't panicked by the thought of doing most of the repairs by myself.

The inspection came and we passed successfully. Although I did most of the work I made sure the employees received their fair share of the credit with the district manager. Slowly the employees came around to my way of thinking. That successful inspection started a three-year run where our Del Taco went from being the 'worst' store in the district to the top store in the entire company.

Although we might not have been the best company store,

Del Taco Supervisor Carson #67 Albert Okura. (1983)

Del Taco Carson #67 Crew Members (1983)

everyone at the corporate office would talk about us and the other Del Tacos would worry about us because I installed such a confident attitude in the store. We backed up our boasts by winning every store incentive program the company rolled out such as suggestive selling contests, Christmas decorating contests, and increased sales contests. I accomplished all the above with the same employees that John originally told me to eliminate. I never fired anybody.

Del Taco was the most enjoyable job I ever had because at this stage of life my leadership abilities had been fine-tuned with age and experience. Nonetheless by 1983 I was ready to move on.

Life Lesson Learned:
With the right leadership and motivation, great things can happen.

12

EL POLLO LOCO – LOST OPPORTUNITY

1981 - I was working at Del Taco in Carson, California. Across the street a new restaurant was being built. Their name was El Pollo Loco and I didn't have any idea who they were or what they sold. The contractor and his helpers came to Del Taco every morning to buy coffee. They had a sense of confidence about them that would lead people to believe that they were a major chain.

On the other hand with their average location and somewhat oddball name that most Americans could not pronounce I assumed that they were going to be another small 'Mexican food' restaurant that eventually goes broke.

After six months of construction El Pollo Loco was ready to open. The contractor invited me to their grand opening. I politely told him that I would go even though I knew I wouldn't. The grand opening took place on a very hot Saturday morning. Customers started lining up two hours before opening and by 10:00 a.m. a line formed halfway around the block. I was surprised and amazed that people would wait in line for two or three hours in the hot summer sun. As I watched the lines of people I calculated that they did more

Albert was inspired to open his own chicken restaurant after discovering El Pollo Loco.

sales in one day than we did all week. By now I couldn't wait to get inside their restaurant to look at their operations – I wanted to see what all the commotion was about! On the fourth day, the lines were short enough for me to try their charbroiled chicken. Walking into the restaurant proved to be a life-altering experience. I didn't know how or when but I knew deep inside that chickens would be my destiny.

The first thing I noticed were ten cooking grills placed by the front windows. This is a great idea because what you see is what you get. The second thing I noticed was chicken after chicken cooking on the grills. What a sight and impression they make on new customers. This was volume cooking at its finest. The third thing I noticed was that El Pollo Loco had a very limited menu. You knew that everyone who stood in line was there to buy charbroiled chicken because that was all they sold. The side orders were rice and beans and tortillas and salsa. Flan was available for desert. Simplicity means a more efficient operation, greater productivity, and of course higher profit margins.

The fourth observation was a negative. Everyone in the

Charbroiled chicken cooking on an open flame grill similar to El Pollo Loco.

restaurant spoke Spanish. I was the only non-Spanish speaking person in the restaurant. Relying on a single ethnic group from a foreign country has to limit long-term growth.

Before El Pollo Loco the only chicken available was fried chicken. I grew up eating hamburgers and fries and never acquired the taste for fried chicken, but El Pollo Loco chicken was something new and delicious. There was no batter, it wasn't fried, and it had a citrus marinade that gave it a zesty taste. I quickly became hooked on El Pollo Loco. I started visiting all of their locations including their original location at McArthur Park, Los Angeles. They all served the same delicious charbroiled chicken. El Pollo Loco had a mystique about it and was rapidly developing a cult following.

In a few short years El Pollo Loco became the hottest restaurant idea in Southern California. Copycat restaurants were popping up everywhere. It seems there was a new charbroiled chicken chain opening every month. El Pollo Loco still led the way.

I was convinced that El Pollo Loco was too ethnic to become a mainstream restaurant chain. The owners probably felt the same way because in 1983, when they were offered a very large sum of money from Denny's Coffee Shop chain to sell their American rights, they quickly sold out.

Although I knew that Denny's was a very large corporation with the capital to help El Pollo Loco expand I doubted if the corporate executives understood the intangible qualities that made them great. I also doubted that any of the executives could successfully operate a fast food charbroiled chicken restaurant.

With the original owners franchising was not available. The first thing Denny's did was set up a franchising program so they could expand. Denny's wanted to sign territorial rights to companies or persons with deep pockets to grow faster. Denny's also 'fine tuned' the menu selection to decrease their food costs and to improve profit margins. They did this by raising prices across the menu board and emphasizing more profitable items such as two-piece and three-piece combo meals. The next thing they did was completely change the recipe! Someone in the corporate office decided they would get Heart Association approval for their chicken because Americans were becoming more health conscious. The way you obtain Heart Association approval is to take all the salt out of your product. I don't think there is any known salt substitute that really tastes like salt. I thought it was humorous when El Pollo Loco put little hearts all over their menu telling you to eat to your heart's content. The new chicken was very bland. Sales plummeted so they were forced to change their recipe again. Unfortunately their recipe was never the same.

The first rule in the restaurant business is to sell something that people will buy with their money. If someone can throw a chicken in the oven, put a little salt and pepper on it and make it taste better than yours, you are in big trouble. The second rule fast food chains need to understand is that people who are really concerned about their health will cook their own food at home or frequent specialized restaurants. They probably won't eat at your restaurant regardless of what you try to tell them.

El Pollo Loco's expansion plans coincided with the booming

1980s real estate market. To secure good locations they were forced to sign higher than average leases. My personal experience is that the real estate market will always go up and down with the economy but leases increase every year. The only two ways to combat increasing leases is to sell high volume or raise prices. El Pollo Loco raised prices. By the early 1990s El Pollo Loco's expansion was in full force. It seems that they were opening everywhere including Las Vegas, San Diego, and the state of Arizona.

The real estate bubble burst about the same time as their new stores were opening up. With so many El Pollo Locos opening in a short period, their brand name and quality of charbroiled chicken was being diluted. Low sales, high prices, high overhead, and lack of experienced cooks created huge losses and closures of many stores. El Pollo Loco was on the verge of bankruptcy.

1999 - Denny's sold El Pollo Loco to American Securities Capital Partners. Under the new ownership El Pollo Loco regrouped and has grown to be a respectable fast food chain. The emphasis is now focused on higher profit items such as Pollo Bowls and Chicken Salads. Charbroiled chicken has become more of a symbol of their past than their future. Once it lost its charbroiled chicken mystique, El Pollo Loco became a shadow of what it could have been. In my opinion, it will always be a regional chain at best.

2005 - El Pollo Loco was sold to Trimaran Capital Partners.

Life Lesson Learned:
If you have a mystique about you or your company you better fight hard to keep it because once it's gone, it's not coming back.

ROTISSERIE vs CHARBROILED

YOU DECIDE

ADVANTAGES

1. Slow cooked over 3 hours to produce a more tender chicken.
2. More moist because natural juices drip to chickens below.
3. Chicken never comes in direct contact with flames.
4. More juices retained means better chicken flavor.

DISADVANTAGES

1. We use more gas because we insist on slow cooking over 3 hours.
2. It takes 2-3 years to train employees how to cook perfect chickens.
3. We have to do more thinking and planning when it comes to rostisserie cooking because we want to serve delicious chicken to everyone.

ADVANTAGES

1. Cooks much faster so it reduces gas bills.
2. Taste best right off the grill because the longer it sits the tougher the meat gets.
3. Easy to cook because you just throw it on the grill and flip it over a couple of times just like your barbecue at home.

DISADVANTAGES

1. Chicken dries out faster be cause it is cooked over an open flame.
2. Chicken is cut open on the grill allowing natural juices to drip into the fires.
3. The chicken burns easily as the flames flare up.

13

OPPORTUNITY IN THE 'INLAND EMPIRE'

1983 - I was thirty-one years old and making four hundred dollars per week working as a manager at Del Taco. I knew that it was time to move on but I wasn't sure what to do.

My cousin Glen Komatsu told me that his Uncle George owned a shopping center in Ontario, California. There was a vacant restaurant available on the property. They thought it would make a perfect charbroiled chicken location considering there was a large Hispanic population in Ontario.

Before Glen told me about the Ontario location I had visited the city once and that was in 1969 to watch a stock car race at the now closed Ontario Motor Speedway. I remember the temperature was over one hundred degrees we got lost in a sandstorm and there was no freeway access.

In the 1970s the 'Inland Empire,' which included Ontario, was known for acres of vineyards, huge citrus farms, numerous dairy farms, hot weather, and unbearable smog. I vowed that I would never move to San Bernardino County.

Ten years later I was ready to go anywhere and do anything

July, 4 1934

Euclid Ave Ontario, Ca Attracted early settlers from the East with it's year-round greenery. (1934)

to succeed. I packed my bags for Ontario and never looked back.

George Komatsu's son Robert, met me at his grocery market in Mira Loma. When he took me to Ontario, I fell in love with the location. Euclid Avenue, originally designed in the 1880s to promote the city, is one of the most beautiful streets in the county. The fifty-foot wide landscaped mediums in the center of the street provided a much needed greenbelt for the shade-deprived area.

I knew this would make a good location for a restaurant.

Life Lesson Learned:
Never say never. You need to go where opportunity lies, it will not come to you.

14

GEORGE KOMATSU – 'THE HUMAN COMPUTER'

I met "Uncle George" Komatsu in 1983. George's brother Ben married my dad's sister so technically George is not my real uncle, but after meeting him I always felt comfortable calling him Uncle George.

George Komatsu was a Japanese-American born in the United States but schooled in Japan. After World War II the Komatsu family farmed hundreds of acres in Arizona growing vegetables and fruit.

George had a falling out with his two brothers Ben and Jimmy so he left for California with nothing but his wife. Needing a job George got into the grocery store business. He didn't know anything about the business but he quickly realized success depended on purchasing power, 'buying deals', product turnover, and theft control. Because he mastered these requirements, he became very successful.

George Komatsu's main store on 6th St. Norco, California.

George reminded me of a human computer. He analyzed everything objectively. He was a numbers man. He was the money-man. With little formal training, he mastered financing, bookkeeping, accounting, banking, tax preparation, buying, and marketing.

I learned from George there were only three ways to legitimately become wealthy in America: 1. Stock market, 2. Real estate, 3. Business. He told me few people understood financials to become wealthy from the stock market and real estate usually took years to accumulate wealth. That left business as the best opportunity for people like me to make money.

George was very meticulous when it came to accounting. He wanted to make sure everything is done according to the tax code. George would take advantage of every legal tax option but he would never stretch the interpretations of the law. He told me that if someone does something wrong but can resolve it by paying a fine it is not a major problem but if you face criminal charges all the money in your bank account might not help you. George was the only man I ever met who could study financials of publicly traded companies and enjoy it. George made a small fortune investing in undervalued stocks.

George Kamatsu, personal assistant Audry, and Armando Parra discuss Ontario grand opening (1983)

By the early 1980s my uncle Ben Komatsu, from Scottsdale, Arizona began buying stock in a charbroiled chicken chain called El Pollo Asado. Knowing George owned a shopping center in Ontario with a vacant restaurant and large Hispanic population he suggested opening a chicken restaurant. George was instrumental at getting Juan Pollo off the ground. He had his son Robert supply the needed capital and was willing to invest whatever was needed. He told me the reason most people failed at business was they did not have enough capital.

Life Lesson Learned:
To start a successful business, you need a financial partner and an operating partner. It is rare for one person to be able to do both.

Armando Parra live broadcast interview by 'Radio 15' - (Jan 1984)

15

ARMANDO PARRA – THE CREATIVE FORCE

Born in Chihuahua, Mexico, Armando Parra immigrated to California with his two young children Michael and Kopitzee. At the time his English was limited so Armando enrolled in an English speaking class. Also taking classes was Indonesia born Linda Oei. Although they made an unlikely couple there was an immediate attraction that led to marriage.

Armando lived in Carson, California close to the Del Taco I was managing. I met Armando because his sister-in-law Gisella Oei lived with the Parras and worked at Del Taco. In 1997 I married Gisella Oei and Armando officially became my brother-in-law. Armando was an interesting person because he was an idea man. He was always looking for a more efficient way to accomplish whatever he was doing. He prided himself on his ability to simplify things. One day Armando came by Del Taco and we talked about the El Pollo Loco across the street. I told Armando how impressed I was with their operations. Armando told me that he had the idea for charbroiled chicken before El Pollo Loco and that in reality they copied him. At the time I took everything he told me with a grain of salt.

Typical rotisserie machine used in Tijuanna, Mexico.

When the opportunity came to open my own charbroiled chicken restaurant I realized I didn't know where to start. Working for the chains did not teach me to be an entrepreneur. Chains do not want independent thinkers because to achieve consistency everyone needs to conform to set rules.

I remembered my earlier conversations with Armando about El Pollo Loco. I called Armando and told him I needed help. Armando took a look at the restaurant and right away told me it was too small to sell charbroiled chicken. The restaurant was built at least twenty-five years earlier as a Winchell's donut shop.

Armando told me we couldn't sell charbroiled chickens because they required too much room with their horizontal barbecue grills. He said I needed to sell rotisserie chicken because rotisserie cookers required much less room plus the fact that all the chicken restaurants 'back in Mexico' sold rotisserie chickens. He claimed El Pollo Loco invented their charbroiled system for America. I told Armando that I needed someone to help convert the restaurant to a rotisserie chicken restaurant. Armando wasn't sure if I was serious but he took the gamble. Before we did anything, Armando took me

Armando Parra cooking the very first chicken. (1983)

to Mexico to look at rotisserie chicken restaurants and see if we could buy cookers. We discovered that equipment made in Mexico was not up to American standards.

After we returned Armando searched all the restaurant supply stores for rotisserie machines. Eventually he found a manufacturer in New York called Old Hickory. We ordered a double sided rotisserie cooker costing eight thousand dollars that could cook up to seventy-two chickens at one time and only took up one-tenth the space of the char-broilers. Although it would take two months to build and ship I was relieved that we found a suitable rotisserie cooker.

The next step was the construction of the new restaurant. I went to the city hall to find out what was required by the officials. I was told to submit a blueprint of the existing layout. I was able to draw the required blueprints because I took two years of drafting in Jr. College. The building department gave me approval to move forward.

I had to submit a similar plan to the County Health Department showing the equipment plan and the sinks and bathrooms. They also approved the plans fairly quickly. The condition of the restaurant was very grim. Armando's first job was demolition. He took out most of the walls, the tile flooring, the fixtures in the restrooms, all the sinks, all the existing signage, the ceiling lights, and most of the broken equipment on the roof.

By the time demolition was complete the building was completely bare. I was a little nervous but I relied on Armando because he sounded so confident. Little by little Armando started putting things back together. I was still confused about where to buy all the equipment and fixtures we needed. When working at the chains you called the commissary and they would send it over with your next delivery. The fast food chains had control over all equipment buys.

1st Ontario location getting ready to open (November 1983)

We started the project in October 1983 and by December we were close to completion. Uncle George told me I had to set a firm date to open otherwise I would get cold feet and never open. We set the date to open the first week in January 1984.

In the meantime I was worried about the rotisserie cooker and cooking the chickens. The cooker we ordered arrived two weeks before our grand opening. Armando figured out how to put the machine together and since I didn't know how to prepare the chicken for cooking I was worried about the recipe. I told Armando he better do something quick! The first thing he did was cook a chicken with

Armando Parra testing the finished chickens. (1983)

no seasoning so he could taste the chicken in its natural state. Armando spent the next week buying a multitude of spices, salts, seasoning, prepared blends of spices, and anything else he could think of to provide flavor. Armando told me that his goal was to enhance the natural flavor of the chicken. He did not want to have an ethnic flavor. He wanted our chicken to spark a memory in people's taste buds of their favorite chicken.

Armando was successful with his marinade. Many customers in the early days claimed it was the best chicken they ever ate! We have not changed our original recipe or cut corners on our marinating process. Armando was always supremely confident of his abilities and it was with good fortune or maybe destiny that I met him.

Life Lesson Learned:
You have to keep your eyes and ears open because the right person may walk into your life.

Albert sampling Armando's first cooked chicken. (December 1983)

Ontario Grand Opening interview with 'Radio 15' (1984)

16

WHAT'S IN A NAME?

The next job we tackled was the name of our business. Since I didn't speak Spanish I asked Armando for his advice. He knew that we wanted to have 'Pollo' in our name because Pollo was Spanish for chicken. Armando suggested the name 'Don Pollo" which translated to Sir Chicken in Spanish. Don Pollo was fine with me so we filed a fictitious business name as required by law.

We opened a checking account and prepared flyers under the name Don Pollo, and then I found out that the name was already being used by a restaurant in Los Angeles. I called Armando and told him we needed to do something quick because there was a potential problem.

We got together to decide a new name. I thought Juan Pollo would be a good substitute because it is similar to Don Pollo, it looks good in print and it sounds noble when spoken.

Next we needed a fictional chicken mascot. A real person might present future problems because unlike Ronald McDonald who could be anywhere at anytime a real person would not be available for multiple appearances.

First Business Card and chicken mascot, designed by Fernando Parra. (1983)

In the case of Kentucky Fried Chicken, Colonel Harland Sanders was the founder of the company and became the face of the company. In order for KFC to grow nationally and maintain profit levels, they had to alter the original recipes. The Colonel didn't understand this so he spent his later years complaining and criticizing the company. They were powerless to stop him because he was a bigger than life living mascot of the chain.

After we agreed on the name and the idea of a mascot, we needed to design a logo and create Juan the fictional mascot. Armando had a solution. He said his brother, Fernando, was an artist and graphic designer. Fernando came up with the cartoon character and designed our logo. Our original logo had the saying, "El Mejor Sabor" or "The best flavor." A few years later, due to popular demand, we changed the saying to "The Best Tasting Chicken."

I believe we ended up with a perfect name for our company. We have a Hispanic name for a Hispanic themed restaurant. We have a fictional cartoon character who represents the company and can be anywhere at anytime.

Life Lesson Learned:
A powerful and great name goes a long way.

17

ROBERT KOMATSU – 'MILLION DOLLAR MAN'

Robert Komatsu got into the grocery business with help from his father. Robert owned Hilltop Market in Mira Loma, California. Located in a blue collar working class area Hilltop proved a challenge for its previous owners.

Robert proved to be a shrewd businessperson. He made sure he fit right in with his customers. To the average person Robert seemed a friendly, naïve, thankful to be there type person. Behind the scenes Robert could be very demanding and at times very eccentric. Because of his home-style approach he developed a large following and made Hilltop Market very profitable even though there was a major chain store one mile down the road.

George and Robert wanted to invest in a chicken restaurant for tax purposes. If the chicken restaurant failed Robert would have a tax write-off for his income taxes. Before I got involved in the actual chicken business Robert was thinking about investing in the Hawaiian shave ice business.

Traditional Hawiian Huli-Huli rotisserie chicken fundraiser. (1983)

George wanted Robert to put his money in the chicken business because he had the location available but Robert was leaning towards a snow cone business modeled after the shave ice businesses in Hawaii.

After I decided to move to the Inland Empire Robert was still debating which business to invest in. I spent my time researching charbroiled chicken and visited every chicken restaurant in the area to study their layout and menus. In the meantime Robert was studying the Hawaiian shave ice business. Robert wanted to get me interested in the shave ice business by taking me to Hawaii so we could personally research the pros and cons of shave ice. I discovered that shave ice is almost a religious experience to those in Hawaii. There are family shops that have a cult following.

Robert had to get back to his business after one week but he told me to stay behind to do more research. I couldn't pass up this offer to stay in Hawaii for two or three weeks. My favorite aunt, Auntie Yuki lived in Honolulu and was happy to let me stay at her house with her family. I stayed in 'Paradise' with cousins Michael and Naomi, went swimming everyday, visited all the tourist areas, bought a used motorcycle and drove all over the Island. I researched

Albert testing Hawiian shave ice at famous Matsumoto grocery store. (1983)

the shaved ice business by eating as much as I could. After three weeks I knew I had to get back to California or I might never come back on my own.

In the 1980s shave ice was becoming a popular fad in Southern California. Robert wanted to cash in on the craze but I was skeptical of the long-term potential of shave ice. Faced with the prospect of extremely high rent beach or tourist locations Robert was hesitant to pull the trigger and open a shave ice shop. He was concerned that his father would not approve if we failed.

I told Robert I wanted to go with the chicken restaurant because it was a safer bet. It proved to be the best decision. Robert became my official partner for Juan Pollo in Ontario. The initial investment was sixty-thousand dollars. Robert was content to be the silent partner. He had little interest in working in the chicken business but he indicated to me that he wanted to let his investment 'ride' if it proved successful. Robert was also my silent partner at the San Bernardino location.

1990 - I had a deal for a third Juan Pollo in Covina. At the time we had a surplus of ninety-thousand dollars in the bank. Robert decided he wanted to have nothing to do with that store. George told me I would have to settle the books with Robert.

ROBERT KOMATSU & Miss Juan Pollo Gina (2002) Riverside Black History Parade

George's accountant informed me I needed to repay the initial investment of sixty-thousand dollars and the remaining thirty-thousand dollars would be split fifty-fifty.

After doing all the work the previous six years I received fifteen thousand dollars and Robert received seventy-five thousand dollars. George told me we were now equal partners. George was right about the business decision so I was not complaining but I made a verbal commitment to the landlord so I decided to keep moving forward. I managed to open the store by borrowing money from my parents and taking a partner Jon Fenley who I knew as a direct mail salesperson from the Ontario store. I knew that partnership troubles were in store for me in the future. My goal was to diversify. A million dollar lawsuit was coming in 2001.

Life Lesson Learned:
Partnerships can become difficult if you are making money.

18

JUAN POLLO #1 OPENS

Before we set the date to open I had to find a place to stay. I couldn't commute everyday from my parents' house and I didn't want to live with Robert at his condominium. I wasn't sure what to do since I didn't have any money for rent. I found a trailer that looked like a small house on wheels. I bought it for five hundred dollars and Armando towed it to Juan Pollo and set it in place behind the restaurant. Now I had a place to stay and a very short walk to work!

Juan Pollo Ontario opened on January 18, 1984. We decided to open without advertising so we could work out bugs before a grand opening. The first day's sales ended up one hundred and sixty-seven dollars. The second day wasn't much better. Sales for the first week totaled two thousand two hundred dollars. Luckily George was more concerned about my getting discouraged and giving up than adding money to cover the bills.

Armando and I were busy figuring out how to get the proper workflow. Armando's plan was to get the employees trained to do specific jobs and have them do the same thing everyday. He was in charge of training the people in the kitchen. I concentrated on personally learning to cook the chicken.

During the first few weeks we were experimenting how to cook the chickens. There were no instructions from the manufacturer on how to cook chicken. There were few rotisserie chicken restaurants open for business. The chicken restaurants we visited in Mexico served chicken that was not that appetizing. To make matters worse I was a lifetime burger man who rarely ate chickens, let alone cooked any.

Ontario, California Grand opening (1984)

Nevertheless I was determined to move forward and learn the chicken business. After we got our feet wet we decided that we needed a grand opening. We decided that a month would be sufficient for learning so we set the date for February 17. I called the local Hispanic radio station and arranged a live broadcast from Juan Pollo.

We needed to come up with a grand opening offer. I thought we should give a half chicken free with the purchase of one whole chicken. George told us we needed a better deal. He felt we needed to have a buy one chicken get one free special. I told him that we couldn't produce enough with that offer. Despite my concerns I gave in and printed grand opening flyers offering one free whole chicken.

Some of the early employees who became Juan Pollo owners.

Jose Garcia

Art Ramirez

Yolanda Campos

Lori Gonzalez

Maria Mora

Cesar Garcia

Celia Martin / Olivia Gonzalez

Pepe Ramos

Juan Pollo Ontario Location 1986

On the day of the grand opening, we stocked up as much food as possible. We marinated all the chicken we could and started cooking early in the morning. The radio station brought out their trailer and started setting up. We set up some booths outside to sell shave ice, hot dogs, and drinks.

We didn't know what to expect. As soon as we opened, people started lining up to buy chickens. The radio station set up and started their live entertainment. The parking lot became jam packed with cars trying to park and people coming over to watch the show. The owner of Southland Market was angry as heck that our customers were parking in the lot we shared and not shopping at his market. He claimed he was losing hundreds of dollars. There was nothing we could do about that so we kept moving forward.

Soon there was a long line of customers. There was no way we could keep up with the orders. We ran out of chicken by noon and the line kept growing. It was a disaster. We never cooked so many chickens at one time so we struggled to keep up with the orders. Most of the chickens came out undercooked so we had to finish cooking them in the microwave. By five in the afternoon there was an hour and a half wait. By seven we stopped taking orders for chickens because everything in the machine was already sold.

George admitted that maybe we shouldn't have given one free chicken. We did the best we could but in the end there were unhappy customers. On the bright side we created much publicity for Juan Pollo and people talked about the huge crowd of people at our grand opening for years afterwards.

Armando stayed on for two or three additional months helping train the employees. He hired a Mexican woman to prepare the salsa, potato salad, rice, and beans. He hired a Mexican cook to be in charge of the marinating process. I concentrated on cooking the chicken. We started having consistency problems with the marinating and the side orders. We mixed a new batch of seasoning with every pot of water and Armando's man sometimes forgot to add the salt resulting in a bland chicken. Armando's food prep woman started coming up with her own variations of the recipes. They didn't speak English and I spoke no Spanish.

In an attempt to increase sales, additional menu items were added which included jello, pudding, hot dogs, french fries, and chicken sandwiches on dinner rolls. These extra items didn't help. It seemed that we threw away more hot dogs than we sold.

I realized if you want something done right you need to do it yourself. I let the two back room employees go. I personally mixed the seasoning, cooked the rice, made the salsa, started the pots of beans, cooked the potatoes, and cooked the chickens. It was important for me to get control of the food preparation procedures before things got out of hand. This also meant cooking the chickens from opening until closing. It was exhausting work but I was committed to go forward.

After our grand opening we never had a sales day over one thousand dollars. Daily sales ranged from six hundred to nine hundred dollars. Nine months later I called Armando and asked for

Bunny Moreno cooking chicken Jan 1984

advice. He came over and said he knew what the problem was; our prices were too low and he suggested we raise them. I was shocked. I always thought cheaper was better. Figuring I had nothing to lose prices were raised. The very next day we did one thousand three hundred dollars. I couldn't believe it! Whether it was luck, coincidence, or Armando's logic, I realized that a change in attitude was the most important ingredient for increased sales.

This experience was the turning point for Juan Pollo. I stopped waiting for things to happen and took a very aggressive approach. This included stepping up quality control, streamlining our menu (no more french fries, jello, hot dogs, etc.) and telling the employees that they needed to be able to increase production every day.

Albert and Sal Ramirez celebrating Juan Pollo 1st year anniversary. (1985)

1985 - This was a year of growth. Sales steadily increased. Our food preparations were being refined and the consistency improved dramatically. January sales for that year totaled seventeen-thousand dollars. By November the sales rose to over thirty-three thousand dollars. At the end of the year I knew that Juan Pollo was the destiny that I have been searching for my whole life.

Life Lesson Learned:
Destiny can guide you to make the right decisions in life.

19

JUAN POLLO #2 OPENS

1985- Things were going well at Juan Pollo Ontario. Sales were up and we were developing a very loyal following of dedicated customers.

A friend told me there was a restaurant location available in San Bernardino, Calif. I went to investigate and the owner of the property Ralph Monge, happened to be there. I explained what my plans were and he became very interested because the restaurant location was originally a char-broiled chicken restaurant. I told Ralph that before he got too excited about my business he better go to Juan Pollo in Ontario and look at our operation because for all he knew I could be lying. I knew that if I got him to Ontario he would get more excited.

Sure enough Ralph became convinced that we would prosper in his building and he offered to give us a very favorable lease of one thousand dollars a month rent which included all of the fixtures. I told Ralph that even though I wanted the deal I was partners with my 'cousin' Robert and needed his approval. I told Uncle George about the offer and told him in my opinion it was a good deal. I told Robert about the deal and his answer was "I'm not sure." He didn't think the location was in a good area for business so he wanted to think it over.

Teenage employees Gloria and Letty learning the chicken business. (1986)

In the meantime Ralph wanted to get his restaurant leased. Ralph started believing it would be easy for him to open his own rotisserie chicken restaurant. When I couldn't get a commitment from Robert one way or the other I told Ralph I would be happy to help him open his own restaurant. I knew how difficult it was to make it in the business but I gave Ralph as much help as I could such as getting him the right equipment and giving him advice on layout. I wanted to stay on good terms because you never know what might happen.

Ralph opened his restaurant and his sales were dismal. After three weeks Ralph called me with a proposition. He told me he couldn't continue with the restaurant because he won a substantial job contract building hangers for the Chino Airport. He made an offer we couldn't refuse. All we had to pay was twenty-two thousand dollars. That was his cost for the equipment. Ralph paid for all the permits to get re-opened, had the building department and health department sign off, clean and detail the entire restaurant, get the

1988 - Typical work day at San Bernardino #2

Juan Pollo #2 5th Street and Mt Vernon San Bernardino, Ca 1987 Crew

walk-in refrigerators, exhaust hoods, and fire systems checked and approved.

This time George didn't consult Robert, he told him we're opening. George went to his bank and had us apply for a twenty-two thousand dollar loan so we didn't have to use our money. The loan was approved. Ralph got his money and we opened in January, 1986. There was no grand opening because we were the third chicken restaurant to open at that location and I didn't think the local population was too excited about another 'outsider' coming into the 'Westside' of San Bernardino to try and make money.

I knew I had to build a solid crew and work on the product in order to win over the local citizens. At the same time I decided to offer 'Buy 1 Chicken – Get 1 Free' every day all day. That came out to two chickens, tortillas, and salsa for $6.39! Even with our super low price we never experienced lines of customers. I believe everyone was skeptical whether we would stay in business. My plan was to weather it out and concentrate on training and supervision. Things changed later in the year when we received our first great review.

Life Lesson Learned:

It pays to keep the door open even if a deal falls through because it may come back to you.

20

BEHIND THE ARCHES

1986 - Juan Pollo #2 opened in San Bernardino. The same year a book by John Love was published called *'Behind the Arches.'* This book told the story of McDonald's Hamburgers and their rise to greatness. The first chapter was titled 'Yes, There Was a McDonald.' In 1948, Dick and Mac McDonald opened the original McDonald's in San Bernardino, California. Within a few years McDonalds became the most successful restaurant in Southern California. Customers lined up daily to buy hamburgers, cheeseburgers, French fries, and shakes.

1953 - Ray Kroc, a salesperson who sold machines that mixed shakes heard about the success of McDonald's. His interest was to find out why McDonalds used so many of his multi-mixer machines on a daily basis when no other customer used more than one.

Ray went to San Bernardino from his office in Chicago to see first hand why McDonald's Hamburgers was so busy. Ray arrived at the restaurant before opening and parked across the street to observe the restaurant in operation. Ray was amazed at what he

McDonald's original location 1398 N. E Street San Bernardino, California

witnessed. McDonald's had a very limited menu and the small building was able to handle customer after customer during the lunch rush.

That day changed Ray's life. He knew instantly that McDonald's was the opportunity he had been searching for his entire life. In 1961, Ray bought out the brothers for 2.7 million dollars and turned McDonald's into the most successful restaurant chain in the world.

After reading the book cover to cover I realized there were three vital components that allowed McDonald's to achieve their greatness. If any one of the three were not present there would be no McDonald's as we know it. Dick and Mac McDonald were the creators. They came up with the concept of mass producing and selling low priced great tasting hamburgers and French fries. They invented the 'Speedee' service system.

Ray Kroc was the visionary who saw the potential of McDonald's and made it work by recruiting the right people, establishing day to day routines, installing and enforcing quality control, and marketing the company to the public as the unofficial restaurant for

Ray Kroc was selling this Multi Mixer Machine when he met the McDonald brothers.

young families.

Harry Sonneborn was the most unknown and probably the most important component of McDonald's success. Harry was Ray Kroc's partner in the early years. He was the financial brains behind the company. He pioneered the lease-option to buy agreements. Harry signed leases with options to buy the property later. When real estate skyrocketed in the 1970s, McDonald's picked up all the options and as a result became one of the largest real estate holding companies in America.

Ray Kroc 'broke the rules' when it came to expanding McDonald's. He did not want McDonald's to become like every other restaurant chain. Ray refused to take well-meaning advice from those in the restaurant business because he realized that they could only take him as far as they have been.

Ray Kroc relied on people on their way up who were willing to buy into his system and willing to work together to achieve financial success. Ray Kroc invested in people. He promoted from within. He made sure franchisees had the best opportunity to make profit by

Original McDonald's location (1948)

passing on all saving from suppliers he kept franchise fees low and he reinvested profits into training programs such as his famous 'Hamburger University.' The McDonald brothers were in the right place at the right time in the history of America but they did not recognize Ray Kroc as the man who could take them into the big time.

Life Lesson Learned:
An opportunity of a lifetime may be right in front of you and if you recognize it you need to take immediate action.

21

NORMAN BAFFREY-FIRST GREAT REVIEW

July 1986 I received a phone call from Norman Baffrey, a food critic who wrote for the local San Bernardino newspaper. He told me Juan Pollo was the best chicken he ever ate and once his huge following discovered us our sales would skyrocket.

I was skeptical about his claims because I assumed that the *San Bernardino Sun* was just a small local paper that few people read. I knew that any publicity was good publicity even if he exaggerated his readership.

Norman was so impressed with our chicken that he insisted on driving down to Ontario to interview me. When I met Norman in person he reminded me of a Marine drill sergeant because of his tattoos and seemingly gruff exterior.

He started the interview by asking me about our rotisserie cookers. He then answered his own question by telling me that rotisserie is the best way to cook chicken because the flames never touch the chicken and the juices drip to the chickens below allowing them to self-baste.

Early photo of food critic Norman Baffrey

Norman really didn't need me present because he continued to answer his own questions before I could speak. I was sure glad that Norman loved our chicken because I could just imagine what he would write if he didn't.

Before Norman's visit, the San Bernardino location was only open for seven months and the sales were mediocre. I was busy trying to assemble and train a crew. George Felix, a young high school student who was very personable and eager to learn quickly became the best cook in the store. He shared my passion for trying to cook a perfect chicken every time.

Norman told me that the only reason he stopped at Juan Pollo was that he was giving his son a ride to a friend's house and he needed to kill time. Since there were no other customers, Norman did not expect much when he ordered a chicken breast. He later told me he couldn't believe how delicious the breast was.

Instead of complimenting George, Norman came back the next evening to order another chicken breast to make sure he didn't

George Felix impressed Norman Baffrey with his perfectly cooked chicken. (1986)

get a 'special' chicken. George cooked the chicken exactly the same and Norman then told him how delicious it was and that he needed to write a review so people would find out about us.

After Norman's interview he told me that he only reviewed fine dining restaurants but he was making an exception for us because he thought so much of our chicken. He again told me we would experience record crowds. I didn't really believe him but I told him that was great news.

Norman's food column came out on Sunday, August 16, 1986. Norman called me at 8:00 a.m. to remind me to cook as fast as I could. Although the San Bernardino location only had one rotisserie cooker, it had a capacity of ninety chickens. Before his review, sales never exceeded one thousand dollars on any Sunday so I figured we could handle up to two thousand dollars easily. I called George to tell him to expect extra customers so make sure he loaded up the machine early.

Since I didn't take Norman's warning seriously I didn't rush to get to the restaurant. I arrived about noon and George had already sold over five hundred dollars! The good news for us was that every table in our dining room was full of customers. The bad news was that they were all waiting for their food because we were out of chickens. In 1986, there were no cell phones so George couldn't call me to tell me to let me know what was going on.

George had the rotisserie cooker full of chickens and had the fires on high so I told him not to worry because it would probably slow down. George looked at me and told me that customers have been telling him that that the lines would get longer as the day progressed – not shorter! By 2:00 p.m., the sales reached one thousand dollars and the wait was over one hour. By now I was getting real nervous. The lines were getting longer and longer and that meant the wait would also get longer. We came up with a plan to tell everyone in line to come back tomorrow and we would give them a complimentary chicken. No sooner did we send the line away than new lines formed. It became a madhouse!

By 6:00 p.m., we had over two thousand dollars and the wait was still long. The customers were asking if we had extra drumsticks for sale so they could try the chicken. I had to turn them down because every chicken in the cooker was sold. Every half hour George would go out into the line and give the free chicken certificate offer but new customers kept coming.

By 7:00 p.m., we stopped taking orders because every chicken in the machine was sold and we couldn't cook anymore before closing. The sales reached twenty-five hundred dollars but we could have easily doubled that if we had chickens to sell.

That Sunday was the most amazing day in Juan Pollo history. Norman's predictions were all true. He had a huge loyal following that could swarm a restaurant with a good review from his column. Norman's readers were not traditional fast food customers. Most were expecting a sit down full serve restaurant. Overnight we obtained his upper middle class customers even though we were located in a low-income neighborhood. Norman's article doubled our monthly sales from about twenty-thousand dollars a month to over forty-thousand dollars a month.

Life Lesson Learned:
Treat every customer as you would your best friend because you never know who might walk in your doors.

SAN BERNARDINO COUNTY
The Sun
SUNDAY/$1
AUGUST 3, 1986
METRO EDITION

This chicken will wing its way into your heart

By NORMAN BAFFREY
Special to The Sun

DINING OUT

Here is the text from Norman Baffrey's food review article:

When it comes to chicken, we have lived with Kentucky Colonel, Pioneer, Church's, Pail O' Chicken and other fast food fowl factories. Then, along came the "spices" -The Crazy Chicken (EL Pollo Loco) with it's Mexican seasonings, and Popeyes with its Cajun touch.

Albert The Chicken Man

Well, its about time to put an end to the controversy over who's better than whom. For my money, Juan Pollo wins - wings-down.

Chicken is one of our most versatile foods, and none of the medical authorities has singled it out as a health threat. In fact, it seems to be a recommended alternative to everything else.

I have had it boiled, broiled, char-broiled, baked, barbecued, sautéed, deep fried, steamed, boned, flattened, rolled, stuffed, shredded, diced, hot and cold - every way but raw. I'll bet just about every national cuisine has its own chicken specialty.

The history of Juan Pollo, not surprisingly, can be traced to Mexico. Albert Okura, who worked for Burger King for eight years and Del Taco for three, visited Mexico with his friend and partner, Armando Parra. The rotisserie method of cooking chicken fascinated Albert.

Following that trip, Armando developed a secret seasoning. So combining the seasoning and the rotisserie method, the men decided to try their luck in the restaurant business. They opened their first store in Ontario in January, 1984.

The partners experimented with various brands of chickens, which have three layers of skin. Most suppliers pluck the feathers and the first layer. Armando and Albert found a company, George's Chicken from Arkansas, that offers daily delivery of fresh birds with the top two layers of skin removed. They are a fairly uniform 3 pounds uncooked, and are less oily than most brands.

To cook the birds they boil water, then add the special seasoning and the chickens, 50 at a time, which are marinated for four hours. A French style rotisserie made by Old Hickory in New York is used to cook the birds.

Eighteen spits, each sporting four birds, flank a central, vertical gas heater. Juices and fat cascade onto other birds below and end in the troth, never sputtering on the flame. The chickens turn slowly for three hours, until they are golden brown.

The result is absolutely the juiciest, tenderest, most succulent chicken I have ever eaten. The marinade penetrates the flesh and spreads it's delicious flavor throughout, not just in the skin. Haven't you always wished the rest of the chicken tasted as good as the first bite? Well, this one does. I was so enamored of this chicken, I went back four times the first week and even drove to Ontario, Ca to meet the owner............................

22

FINDING THE PERFECT CHICKENS

Because 100% ground beef hamburger is the same regardless of the producer I assumed the same principle applied to chickens. My belief that all chickens were created equal was wrong. I also didn't know anything about the chicken distribution methods so we bought chickens from the company (Zacky Farms) used by Robert at his Hilltop Market. I learned later that the price they charged us was more than we could have gotten elsewhere.

Since Robert briefly owned a fried chicken restaurant in Arizona he suggested we use a two pound twelve ounce chicken but after six months it was evident that they were too small for our needs because there wasn't enough meat on the wings and drumsticks. Fried chicken is coated with batter so the wings and drumsticks looked much bigger after cooking.

A slightly larger chicken made a big difference for us. We increased to a three pound two ounce chicken which has proven to be our ideal size. Since the bone structure stayed relatively the same the additional weight was all meat.

Bigger is not always better. If we use bigger chickens they are

Pancho stacks 60 cases of George's Inc. chicken in the walk-in
preparing for typical weekend sales in San Bernardino, Ca (1987)

more difficult to cook because they need to be cooked much longer
and the marinade cannot penetrate the entire breast.

During the first year there would be times that the chickens in the warmer would start to smell like fish. I grew up eating fish every friday but I never saw fish that looked like a chicken. Our chicken distributor explained that some growers add fish meal to their chicken feed and the odor will bleed through after cooking. The best tasting chickens are corn fed.

We still had a problem with consistency. Sometimes the chicken would taste delicious and the meat would be full of flavor and sometimes the chickens would taste bland and be dry. I was cooking the chickens the same way everyday and they were all marinated with the same recipe.

Albert holding George's Inc. brand 3lb 2oz chicken. (1988)

One day I thought it might be the brand of chicken. Our new chicken distributor supplied us with George's Inc. chicken most of the time and other brands the rest of the time. It seemed that every time we used George's Inc., the chicken tasted better. I began to pay close attention and realized there was a big difference in the George's chicken and the other brands we were using.

I had no idea why their chicken cooked better but I made a point to request only George's. They were impressed that I insisted on their brand so they flew me to their modern processing plant in Arkansas and gave me a personal tour.

I discovered reasons their chickens worked so well in our system and others didn't. Besides being corn fed for most of their lives they used a higher scalding temperature when processing that removed not only the feathers but extra layers of fat from the skin. The result was a chicken that did not have a greasy feel to the skin.

George's Inc. chicken fit into the Juan Pollo family. 1984 Ontario original crew members as viewed through the eyes of Albert Okura. Five now own their own chicken restaurants. (2012)

Our marinating process consists of hot marinade poured over the raw chickens. The hot marinade opens the pores in the skin to allow the seasoning to penetrate into the meat. We leave it marinating overnight. The citric juices in the marinade help tenderize the meat. Most chicken growers do not scald as hot when processing and there may be several reasons. First, they sell chickens by the pound and extra fat on the skin helps increase the weight. Second, when these chickens are packaged to sell at the markets, the extra fat gives the chickens a golden color that makes them look very appetizing. Fat on the skin blocks the marinade from penetrating into the breast meat and leaves the skin greasy after cooking.

Life Lesson Learned:
Contrary to what I thought, 'chicken is chicken' is not always true.

23

COOKING THE PERFECT CHICKEN

Cooking the perfect rotisserie chicken is an art. I discovered that it takes up to five years to teach someone to become an expert on cooking rotisserie chickens using these cookers. The secret is being able to cook for low sales days, medium sales days, holidays, very high sales days, and party order days.

1983 - I did not know how to cook chicken, especially with a rotisserie cooker. There was no written instruction on cooking because very few restaurants specialized in rotisserie chickens and the ones that did sell rotisserie chickens generally relied on a special sauce to smother the chickens with flavor.

Since 1984, I have relied on trial and error to master the cooking process. This includes personally cooking thousands of chickens over a variety of conditions. I have learned to cook any amount of chickens at any time on any day. This ability to cook chickens on demand and cook them correctly separates us from the competition.

There are no restaurant chains or independent restaurants that have the potential or ability to duplicate what we do.

Armando Parra helped me get into the rotisserie business

Kyle and Aaron serving perfect chicken.

and together we learned the basics of cooking rotisserie chickens. At the beginning we numbered every spit. We wrote down the time we put them in the cooker. We then attempted to cook each spit for two hours.

We learned if you left the spits in the same position for two hours the top spits would be overcooked and the bottom spits would still be raw. Vertical rotisserie cookers such as as ours do not circulate heat throughout the machines so the heat rises to the top and cooks faster if the chickens are allowed to stay there.

The next step was to move the spits around to get them to cook more evenly. We still had to write down the time each spit was put into the cooker. This wasn't that efficient because if a cook forgot to log the time down, the next cook would have to guess which were cooking the longest.

Finally we started loading all the new spits at the bottom of the cookers and rotated them towards the top as chickens were done. This kept the chickens in the correct order so anyone could take over the cooking and know that the oldest chickens were the ones at the top.

I discovered the ideal cooking time for our chickens is three hours. The chickens cooked much better when they were loaded at the bottom because they started at a much lower cooking temperature. The slower the chicken cooks at the beginning, the tenderer it becomes as it is cooked. At lower initial temperatures the juices stay inside the chickens allowing the juices to keep the meat moist.

When a cook starts the spit at high temperatures the heat causes the juices to burst out of the pores in the skin. These juices will be gone forever and generally results in a dry flavorless product. If the chicken starts cooking at a lower temperature the pores of the skin stay closed and the natural juices stay inside.

The most important aspect in cooking the chicken correctly is proper timing because we never know when customers will walk in the door and we don't know how big an order they want. Cooks need to be able to adjust cooking times depending on sales and that means cooking anywhere from two hours to five hours. Perfectly cooked chickens will translate into more sales and more profits.

It takes about three years for a cook to experience every situation needed to be able to handle any sales day. Unlike other fast food systems where every menu item is cooked the same way every time there are three distinct methods of cooking that Juan Pollo owners and managers need to master.

1. New or inexperienced method. New cooks need a large cushion of chickens cooking at lower temperatures so they have time to load and unload cooked chickens. It takes time and experience for cooks to be able to handle chickens without damaging them. Cooked chickens that are done can be burned five minutes later if not taken out on time.

It takes 2-3 years to become proficient at cooking the chicken. Eric has been cooking over 12 years in San Bernardino. (2007)

2. Experienced method. Experienced cooks have the ability to run higher temperatures and smaller cushions of chickens cooking because they have the ability to take chickens in and out of the machines efficiently. Depending on the time of day a good cook will keep a certain amount of cooked chicken in the warmers and have enough chickens cooking for the next three or four hours. Chickens in the machine need to be kept at a 'Dark-Medium-Light' condition which allows a steady flow of cooked chickens. If it gets busy temperatures can be raised to cook faster and if it is slow temperatures can be lowered.

3. Emergency cooking method. Generally this is 'panic' cooking. There are times the store runs out of chickens because more are sold than anticipated. Usually this happens when cooks get complacent and fail to load up enough new chickens for later sales. The natural tendency is to turn fires full blast, burn the skin, cut the chicken, and serve it to the customer. Emergency cooking can make the difference between increasing sales and decreasing sales. Customers

Albert has become the foremost expert on cooking rotisserie chicken by personally cooking over one million chickens.

FIGURE: 23 years = 1196 weeks = 8372 days x 120 (Average amount of chickens Albert cooked per day) = 1,004,640 Chickens. No one in America has cooked more chicken within this time frame. (1984-2007)

who receive chicken that is rushed without consideration of quality will think twice before coming back. The secret to emergency cooking is to cook the chickens as fast as you can without serving them raw or burned. After chickens are 80% cooked the flames need to be lowered to allow the chicken to finish the cooking at a slower pace.

Sella Okura demostrates the proper method of cooking "Dark-Medium-Light"

It is better to have the customers wait an additional ten to fifteen minutes and get a well cooked chicken than have someone rush and serve chickens that aren't quite done. The problem with emergency cooking is that employees don't always understand why they ran out in the first place and they will repeat their mistakes over and over. Rushed cooking will never taste as good as normal cooking.

The growth of the Juan Pollo brand will ultimately depend on our ability to improve our consistency in cooking perfect chickens.

Life Lesson Learned:

If you can master cooking perfect chickens and train others, there is unlimited future in the rotisserie chicken business.

24

PAYING MY DUES

When I decided to open my own business in 1983 I was thirty-one years old and determined to stick it out the next five years no matter what happened. I decided to do whatever it took to be successful. That meant working open to close daily. I started the chicken at 7a.m. and worked until 11p.m. closing.

In order for me to set the tone of the company and apply my belief that the best person qualified should always be the boss I had to be the best worker, the best cook, the best leader. I learned this in middle school when I read about Charles Darwin and his *Theory of Evolution.* I knew he based his theory on 'survival of the fittest,' the strong survived and the weak perished.

I worked harder and longer than I ever did before. It seemed that every year I was working more because the sales climbed so fast but I feel I thrived and prospered because I had mentally prepared for this opportunity.

Earlier in my life I vowed to never again mentally burn out because that always leads to physical burnout. When people would

Albert Okura paying his dues in the 1980s.

ask me how I could work so hard and so many hours, I always told them this wasn't a job it was the game of life and I was competing to win. If I counted the hours I know I would have burned out.

After opening the second store thirty miles away in San Bernardino, I was driving back and forth sometimes three times a day. There were many times I was so tired, I had to pull off the freeway and take a nap. By the late 1980s the weekends were so busy that we had to start cooking hundreds of chickens at 6:00 a.m. just to keep up with the sales. Everyone would be exhausted by the end of the weekend because cooking rotisserie chickens at high temperatures and at high speeds is physically draining. Every Monday the routine started over. I always wanted to make sure that I looked refreshed and ready to go no matter how exhausting the weekend was. I discovered the secret was to pretend the hectic weekend never took place. That way I could never complain about being too tired.

Albert's one bedroom house trailer behind the restaurant. (1985)

The first two years at Ontario, I lived in a house trailer Armando installed ten feet from the back door. Every morning I had to start cooking the chickens. Four times a week the sound of the chicken delivery truck would wake me up early in the morning. I would have to get up, get dressed, open the delivery door, and carry each box of chicken into our walk in cooler.

The chicken distributor told me that the early delivery was the only time they could deliver unless we were willing to be on the return route which meant the cases would be on the truck over fourteen hours. It took two years to find a local chicken distributor who would come at a more reasonable time. I did get revenge on the original chicken supplier because when they later discovered how much chicken the Ontario location was selling they started calling and pleading to let them become our distributor again.

Life Lesson Learned:
The restaurant business is 'Survival of the Fittest' and you get what you deserve in the end.

Working hard in 2000.

25

JUAN POLLO COVINA – SECOND GREAT REVIEW

During the late 1980s, I met Jon Fenly, an advertising sales representative who worked for the direct mail company that printed and mailed coupons for us. He became enamored with the idea of Juan Pollo rotisserie chicken and wanted to open his own store. I was skeptical because I knew that salesmanship alone will only take you so far in business.

1990 - Jon found a location for rent in the city of Covina, California. It used to be a Kentucky Fried Chicken restaurant. They moved to a better location that had better visibility from the street. John was very excited about the location but I told him that I was partners with Robert and at this point couldn't make a separate deal.

After Robert decided he didn't want to be partners in Covina and the money in our account was divided I took Jon as my partner and signed a ten-year lease.

The restaurant was in very poor condition after all those years of serving fried chicken. Jon took it upon himself to do the complete refurbishing of the restaurant. Jon set a goal of remodeling and opening one month after signing the lease.

Jon Fenly directing the remodeling of Covina restaurant (1990)

Jon not only had to have architectural plans drawn and approved he had to completely redo the plumbing, electrical, roofing, and walls, clean and repair twenty feet of exhaust hoods, add a produce walk-in, install all equipment, and install all new ceramic tile flooring, and get health department and building department approvals within a four week period.

Jon amazed me. He used his salesmanship charm to get every official on his bandwagon to help get us open. He operated the telephones from morning to night pleading, begging, directing, organizing, demanding, or wheeling and dealing. The outcome was that Jon got us open within his self imposed deadline and got it accomplished with all appropriate fees, permits, and approvals.

I learned that the secret to being a good contractor is not necessarily your work experience or even your knowledge, but being able to set your daily or weekly objectives, simultaneously tackle multiple responsibilities, find sub contractors that will get the results you need, and personally follow up every detail. No Juan Pollo has ever opened in less time.

Covina owner Hartoyo Gandasetiawan and his crew. (1995)

Planning a grand opening went quick. Armando Parra wanted us to hire the #1 'Hispanic' DJ in Los Angeles, Humberto Luna to do a live remote. Recalling the success of our original grand opening event Armando felt that we would have longer lines of customers because Humberto was such a huge celebrity. Although his price seemed excessive at ten thousand dollars I took the gamble that we would have record crowds.

On the grand opening day we were ready for anything. We cooked hundreds of chickens and stocked up a walk-in full of salsa, potato salad, rice, and beans. Humberto's radio station came out at 10:00 a.m. to set up their promotional vehicle and bring their entertainment.

Unfortunately few people showed up. The event was a bust. Even though Humberto was in his studio urging everyone to come to Juan Pollo Covina to get free chicken, no one seemed to be paying attention. There were more employees than paying customers.

The situation got worse as the day went on. By the time we

SAN GABRIEL VALLEY

Tribune

NOVEMBER 29, 1991

VALLEY
Cities offer
remap plan
7 supervisors?
/ B1

PLENTY TO CLUCK ABOUT

DINING

Juan Pollo: Covina restaurant manager Martin Ramirez removes chicken from the vertical rotisserie.
John Fontes / staff photographer

Pollo Loco, Juan Pollo make chicken a fast-food treat

By Peg Rahn
Restaurant Writer

REVIEW

A visit to two of our local fast-food places that feature only chicken makes it clear that the sky is falling.

It's coming down in a shower of money for the franchise owners. And for good reason. Their narrow focus on chicken with (sides) allows them to concentrate on doing it right.

Appropriately, Pollo Loco (crazy chicken) started the craze in the Los Angeles area. The chain has made a real effort to be consistent. I visited three different locations and found them all clean, efficient and having the same quality.

While Pollo Loco may have begun the idea, the owners of Juan Pollo have perfected it. Before launching their fast-food variation-on-a-theme, Albert Okura and Armando Parra spend a lot of time on research on how to improve on the pack leader. And they have.

At their San Bernardino location alone, they sell more than six tons of moist, succulent, large and tender pieces of chicken a week! And that doesn't count the stores in Covina, Ontario and Rancho Cucamonga.

The vertical grill sets the Juan Pollo chicken apart. Its marinated chicken has a more natural taste than Pollo Loco, and the chickens aren't bright yellow.

Juan Pollo uses only chickens from the South. No oil is added because the chickens naturally baste each other as they revolve slowly in the vertical grill for five hours.

The pieces are huge and the skin (they have removed two of the three layers that chickens have to make them less fatty) is delicious. Of course, you can remove it if you want to eliminate more fat.

The (sides) at Juan Pollo taste homemade, with no artificial packaged spice taste. Everything is made from

El Pollo Loco

Where: Check your telephone directory for the closest location in the San Gabriel Valley

When: Hours vary with location

How much: Prices are reasonable, at $1.89 for a burrito, $1.99 for 2 pieces of chicken with only a tortilla and salsa ($3.09 if you want two sides), or $3.01 for one of the new sandwiches. No credit cards or checks.

The food: El Pollo Loco locations are clean, efficient and pleasant places to catch a quick bite or take-out. The food is simple, but the chicken and rice have a bit too much of a (package) spice mild taste to suit me as a regular diet.

Libations: No alcohol

Info: Check your telephone directory or call corporate headquarters (909) 885-6324 for the nearest location.

Juan Pollo

Where: 349 W. Covina Blvd., Covina (also in San Bernardino, Ontario and Rancho Cucamonga)

When: 9 a.m. to 10 p.m. daily

How much: Inexpensive. Prices range from $1.10 for tacos, to $2.25 for a humongous burrito and sides to $7.99 for a whole chicken. No checks or credit cards.

The food: Huge portions of succulent, delicious chicken make Juan Pollo a place for anyone who loves chicken. It is basically a take-out place with a few tables so there's not much atmosphere. Service is fast and the menu is All-American with a Mexican twist. Each of the sides is well-seasoned. If you're a regular, Juan Pollo offers incentives of 2-for-1 or the lunch card as a bonus. The food is so good, you don't need a bonus!

Libations: No alcohol.
Info: (818) 858-0609.

scratch, including the fresh salsa. Sides include corn on the cob, potato salad and beans. Even the flour tortillas have a savory taste.

This chicken is so moist that you can order it by whole pieces ($3.75 for 2 pieces with two sides, tortillas and salsa) or in tacos ($1.10) or the gigantic chicken burrito ($2.25).

Juan Pollo also offers 2-for-1 incentives as well as a ilunchi card that earns the customer a free lunch after 10 paid lunches.

El Pollo Loco, nonetheless, has its place. Many put the grill near the order counter so the customer can watch the chicken being grilled. Personally, the bright yellow color (from tumeric in the marinade) of the chickens turned me off. It makes them look like rubber chickens.

But the taste was all right. Select the whole pieces as opposed to ordering dishes that have the chicken cut up if you want the juciest fowl. The menu board has red heart labels next the the best nutritional bets.

The two-piece combo with rice (too much seasoned salt), Mexican beans and corn tortillas makes a nice lunch for only $3.29. There are serving sizes that go up to 8-12 pieces for $7.99. Regular sides are corn on the cob, Spanish rice, pinto beans, potato salad and cole slaw. Garden salad also available for an extra $1.29.

Other choices are burritos (dry chicken) or three new sandwiches. The Pueblo with chilies and cheese has a nice zip to it. The Teriyaki is the big favorite of the PCC location, and the Premiere has honey dijon mustard to round it out.

Look for the new fax-able menus to appear shortly, another service to make Pollo Loco even easier to eat.

View complete text of this article on juanpollo.com

closed there was so much food left over that we could have fed a small army. We were very disappointed because there was no return on our advertising investment. What I learned was you never know what will happen at any given time with media and media personalities. Sometimes you strike it big – as our grand opening in Ontario, and sometimes you strike out – as Covina did.

After our grand opening fiasco the Covina store settled into an average sales routine. Most new restaurants open with crowds of curious customers and hit rock bottom within one or two months. How you handle the bottom determines the future of the restaurant. Restaurants that are undercapitalized start cutting back on advertising, payroll, and food quality. Restaurants that survive long term keep their standards and absorb the losses until sales turn around.

Jon enjoyed the fast pace of wheeling and dealing with vendors and contractors. He was eager to open more restaurants. Slugging it out on a daily basis became a grind for John. The day to day routine with low sales became more than he could handle so John left. When he left I took another partner but it ended a short time later with the same results.

At this point I decided to send one of my cooks, Martin Ramirez from the Ontario location to help stabilize the store. Martin made the drive everyday and started learning to help manage the store since I didn't have a working partner. Although we never made any money while Martin was cooking, my plan was to build a loyal customer base.

In November 1991, I received a call from the *San Gabriel Valley Tribune*. They only told me that they wanted to go to the Covina store and take a photo of the chicken. I figured any publicity in the newspaper would be good.

On November 29, 1991 there was a big picture of Martin cooking the chicken along with a review of El Pollo Loco versus Juan Pollo. If I didn't know any better the article sounded like the writer

Peg Rahn, wrote a commercial for Juan Pollo! She starts by telling how El Pollo Loco started the chicken craze and how the Juan Pollo owners perfected it. Our chicken is described as succulent, moist and delicious. Peg avoided talking about El Pollo Loco's food quality and when she did, it wasn't too complimentary. "The bright yellow color of the chickens turned me off" because they "look like rubber chickens," and the best she could say about their chicken was "the taste was all right."

Although Peg's review did not create lines of customers like Norman Baffrey's did, this was an unsolicited review that directly compared us with El Pollo Loco and praised everything we were doing and had few good things to report about El Pollo Loco.

Martin later went on to open his own Juan Pollo in Bloomington, California.

Life Lesson Learned:
In this business, we are the experts in cooking rotisserie chicken. We have to stay vigilant with the quality because you never know who is buying our chicken and what they will write!

26

50 YEAR PLAN

1990 - Receiving weekly and sometimes daily requests for franchise information created a log jam of people coming to the restaurant seeking my help. Rather than just brush callers away, I tried to meet with everyone and personally talk to them so they would rave about us to their friends. Talking for an hour or longer about the chicken business made it impossible for the average person to remember every thing discussed so I prepared a small pamphlet of Juan Pollo newspaper articles which also included my personal beliefs. Most people who came to me were good people but traditional franchising was not available because I did not have proper corporate structure. Those who approached me were looking for and needed direction. It is my opinion that people who have the ability to open their own business seldom seek a franchise.

1992- Most small businesses have a five year business plan if at all. Wanting to stand out in the crowd and to give people hope that one day we would franchise, I put into writing my business plan for the next 50 years.

I got the idea for a fifty year business plan from studying Japanese companies. One of the traits of the Japanese culture is persistence. They can wait years to accomplish seemingly simple goals. Japanese companies always had a fifty-year plan in place.

The restaurant business is a people business. My fifty-year plan will move faster or slower depending on getting the right people in place that can take the company forward. There are four types of people needed to achieve my goals.

The first is the visionary and founder, the lightening rod for the company.

The second group consists of the individuals that share the same vision and have it in them to see the potential of Juan Pollo and have the leadership ability to take this company into the big time. The success of Juan Pollo depends on the ability of its key people to share ideas as a team and at the same time function independently taking care of different responsibilities. The rewards awaiting the right person are unlimited.

The third group consists of mid-level professionals that want to be part of the growth, understand and implement rules and regulations, train and motivate the fourth group.

The fourth group consists of the day-to-day operators such as the unit supervisors, night managers, crew leaders, and crewmembers. This group is the nuts and bolts of the company.

If I get the right people in place I can move fast. If not I will wait for them to join. When I wrote my fifty-year plan there were some parts that were out of my control but have fallen into place. For example, Communism was the biggest threat to world peace and the 'cold war' made it impossible to do business in countries such as China. Over the past two decades communist countries have begun to embrace capitalism while America is becoming more socialist. With the explosion of computer technology and the Internet young people all over the world are learning English. We have instantaneous communication which allows free exchange of ideas. America was the wealthiest nation in the world but after years of uncontrolled illegal immigration and its drain on our resources, America is falling back into the pack and we may be heading to a truly global economy.

Everything seems to be falling into place that would allow Juan Pollo to become a huge restaurant chain. Regardless of changes in technology or social changes, people all over the world will eat chickens. The sensations of sight, smell, and the taste of food can never be replaced.

I believe we are in the right place at the right time in the history of the world.

Life Lesson Learned:
Putting in writing what you plan to do in the future is like putting your money where your mouth is.

This is Albert's fifty year plan as he typed it in 1992 : ------->

```
                        FUTURE PLANS                        page 1.
```

I have followed fast food chains very closely during the past 10 years. There seems to be a desire for a "magical" 5 year plan.

TYPICAL PLAN

Year 1. Get idea, get investors, open prototype, determine menu and operations for maximum profit.

Year 2. Open 1 or 2 more restaurants to give chain status.

Year 3. Go public – raise couple million dollars. Start selling franchises using new capital for advertising and P.R.

Year 4. Franchises start opening nationwide.

Year 5. Sell out to big corporation for big profits.

Almost everyone who followed this path has failed by year 4. I believe there are 2 main reasons for failure:

1. Never spend the time to develop quality product – thus a loyal customer base.
2. Lack "the visionary" to lead and drive the company into the big time (such as Ray Kroc or Colonel Sanders)

For an ordinary person like me, I don't think there are shortcuts to long term success. I have a 50 year plan.

1993 – 2000   1. Continue to open restaurants as opportunity arises.
Age 40's   2. Utilize existing locations to keep costs low.
                3. Pass on savings to customers.
                4. Emphasis on building customer loyalty & awareness.
                5. Build reputation as "Best Tasting" chicken.
                6. Refine operating proceedures.
                7. Develop and put to use operating manual.
                8. Start to design own line of cooking equipment.
                9. Promote from within.

2000 – 2010   1. Develop prototype store.
Age 50's   2. Step up to "chain type" standards of operation.
                3. Become regional chain similar to Carls Jr. or In N Out Burger.
                4. Develop training center to start attracting people from different backgrounds to help stimulate growth – offer benefit package.
                5. Continue to promote from within.
                6. Increase profit margins by reducing costs and more efficient purchasing.
                7. Expand through company owned stores and working partners – investors.
                8. Begin manufacturing of own equipment line of rotissetie cookers.
                9. Begin to become recognized spokesman for company.

future plans....   page 2.

2010 - 2020   1. Become national chain.
  Age 60's   2. Major growth through franchising.
              3. Offer lowest franchise fees possible.
              4. Offer lowest royalties possible.
              5. Help franchisees make as much profit as possible to encourage
                 word of mouth advertising for investors.
              6. Increase purchasing power through volume. Pass savings along
                 to franchisees.
              7. Become recognized as figure head and founder of company. Need
                 to start becoming "larger than life". Purpose will be evident
                 during next 20 years.

2020 - 2030   1. Continue growth through franchising.
  Age 70's   2. Begin to look to overseas for expansion.
              3. Greatest potential for our product is outside of America.
              4. Unlike other food products such as hamburgers, tacos, pizza,
                 fried chicken - every country in the world can identify with
                 rotisserie cooked chickens.
              5. Intend to take advantage of this remarkable situation.
              6. Set up franchise arrangements in most major areas of the world
                 - South America, Europe, Middle East, Far East, etc.
              7. In order to maintain control of Juan Pollo and stay in power to
                 accomplish my goals, I need to become so closely identified with
                 the company that we become synonymous similar to Walt Disney and
                 Disneyland.

2030 - 2050   1. Expand foreign markets.
  Age 80's   2. Expansion to be similar to America plans.
   to 90's   3. Charge lowest royalties and fees possible.
              4. Stress quality of product.
              5. Take American technology of raising chickens throughout the
                 world.
              6. Will benefit countries involved - plus insure company has steady
                 supply of chickens.
              7. Concentrate expansion into mainland China.
                 1.1 billion Chinese - biggest potential market in the world.
              8. Also concentrate in India - population 800 million - due to
                 religious belief, most do not eat beef products.
              9. Always adapt price structures and minor details to suit each
                 particular nation - give customers what they want - not what I
                 want.

2050   Become the #1 seller of chicken in the world.
99 Years Old

2051   Happy old man!
100 Yrs Old

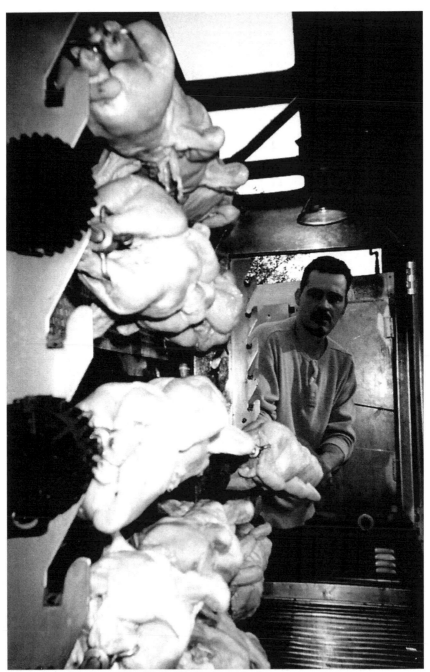

50 year plan is based on cooking 'Perfect' Rotisserie Chicken's.

27

CHINO RESTAURANT SUPPLY

After 1990, I knew I would eventually have problems with Robert Komatsu. I would be in bad shape financially if he pursued legal action. I also had a choice to make: keep two stores and turn them into landmark rotisserie chicken restaurants or taking the much more difficult task of building a major chain and going into the big time.

The path I chose was to go into the big time. My belief was I will succeed or I will go broke. There wasn't going to be middle ground. Although I have been working hard to reach my goals the result is yet to be determined.

To lay the groundwork to be a major company I knew that I had to first create a buffer zone between myself and Robert. This could be accomplished by establishing a parent company to supply goods to the Juan Pollo restaurants. Being the main supplier to a major successful chain is a guaranteed way to be profitable. That role includes supplying food items, proprietary goods, paper goods, specialized equipment, accounting, technical advice, or whatever is needed at the restaurant level.

Chino Restaurant Supply Warehouse - San Bernardino, California (2012)

Chino Restaurant Supply was established to serve the Juan Pollo restaurants. Because we were not an official franchising company in 1992 buys had to be voluntary. The early years were difficult because there wasn't surplus capital to build up inventory. We made most of our money from mixing seasoning bags and selling them to the restaurants and by charging seven cents per pound surcharge on the chickens delivered to the stores.

2001 - Chino Restaurant Supply was self sufficient and showing profit – just in time for the coming lawsuit.

Life Lesson Learned:
In the end companies such as Juan Pollo Inc. will make more money supplying goods and services than running individual restaurants.

28

EXPANSION FROM WITHIN

The 1990s and early 2000s was a time for Juan Pollo expansion. Most of the original employees from Ontario and San Bernardino wanted to open their own restaurants. San Bernardino County grew dramatically in the 1980s. It was difficult to open new restaurants during the booming Ronald Reagan presidency because commercial real estate prices were escalating at unreasonable rates. Landlords and leasing agents were signing leases with tenants before shopping centers were built. When inquiring about rental rates I would be told there was no negotiating because if we didn't move quickly it would be rented to someone else.

I told landlords and leasing agents that whoever signed these leases were going to go broke but they didn't know it. Besides high initial rent there were yearly increases of 5%-6%. I told them to call me after their tenants filed bankruptcy. Most did not appreciate my comments.

1990 - The real estate bubble burst. I had just bought my house in Chino, California for $300,000. By 1991 the value of my house fell below $200,000. A few years later the commercial market

Jose Garcia and brother Caesar Garcia at South Pomona grand opening (1999)

fell. Shopping centers were losing tenants left and right. Many new shopping centers went into foreclosure or were never finished.

After opening Rancho Cucamonga (1990), Covina (1990), and Lake Elsinore (1991), landlords started calling me to lease their locations.

As the tables turned to favor tenants I started playing hard to get and took advantage of the bad economy by making low-ball offers. The La Habra location was our first location in Orange County. The owner of the property, Mr. Charles Patel, personally called to tell me he had a fully equipped rotisserie chicken restaurant for lease. The restaurant was originally a Pioneer Chicken restaurant converted into a copycat Juan Pollo restaurant called "Roastin Pollo."

I told Mr. Patel that we couldn't take over the location for two reasons. First, the previous owner ruined the reputation for rotisserie chickens. Second, the restaurant was located on the busiest street in Orange County (Harbor Blvd.) so the rent would be too expensive. The more I told him I couldn't do a deal the more he insisted I make an offer. Finally, I wrote a ten year lease with starting rent at sixty cents a square foot with gradual increases to one dollar per square foot. The equipment was to be included in the deal. To my surprise, he accepted the offer without any changes.

Ruben Campos Redlands Juan Pollo owner. (2000)

I needed to find someone who wanted to take advantage of the deal. Jose Garcia, one of the original employees from the Ontario location found out and he jumped at the opportunity to own his own store. Since he started working when he was fifteen years old, he had plenty of experience. Jose's spouse, Yolanda, was also an original employee at Ontario. Together, they overcame the previous owner's bad reputation and quickly built sales to a comfortable level. They worked hard and the sales kept rising. They have since opened 5 additional restaurants.

1993 - I received a call to rent a location in Redlands, California. The shopping center was in bankruptcy and there was an 80% vacancy. The leasing agent representing the bank told me he needed Juan Pollo as the anchor tenant so the property would be easier to sell. He told me to write my own lease. I told him I was busy with the existing stores and Chino Restaurant Supply so I needed one year free rent, fifty cents per square foot rent the second year followed by small increases the next eight years. He took the offer.

After two years, I turned the store over to Ruben Campos and his wife Martha, both former employees at the Ontario location in the 1980s. Although both Ruben and Martha were hard workers at Juan Pollo, Ruben's personal problems resulted in a divorce and heavy debts to Chino Restaurant Supply. Ruben changed the name

Chino Town Square Juan Pollo (1995)

to King Pollo after I told him he could no longer be Juan Pollo.

1994 - Terry Bortnik, property manager for Chino Town Square Center introduced himself and told me he wanted Juan Pollo in his center. This location was less than one mile from my house and was an existing restaurant which needed extensive remodeling. I told Terry I was interested because of the location but I needed tenant improvement money and six months' free rent or I suggested he rent to someone else first and call me after they went broke. Terry said he didn't play that game and couldn't give us tenant improvement allowance so I passed on the deal.

Terry rented the location as a juice bar. They invested money, fixed all the damaged areas, installed counters and tile flooring and went broke after three months. I called Terry and told him I was ready to rent the location for a ten-year lease and a smaller tenant improvement allowance. He said he was waiting for my call. We signed the lease and my wife took over the store.

Margaret and Art Ramirez owners of Fontana Juan Pollo (2000)

1996 - I received a call regarding a location in San Bernardino halfway between our Fifth and Mt. Vernon location and an existing Juan Pollo two miles to the east in Highland. The owner Ted Nicolay, wanted us to open a Juan Pollo because he was tired of revolving tenants the past ten years. Everyone who rented the building went broke after one year.

I told Ted's agent that I didn't have time to renovate the building because I was so busy. Ted insisted we rent the space. My response offer was a ten-year lease, the first year free, the second at thirty cents a square foot, and small increases each subsequent year. Ted took the offer.

1995 - Art Ramirez and his wife Margaret were managing Chino Restaurant Supply. Margaret ran Chino Restaurant Supply and did the bookkeeping for the individual Juan Pollos. Art was in charge of distributing goods to the stores. Margaret along with her sister Celia were the first two employees hired at Ontario. Art started working at Juan Pollo as a teenager because he was interested in dating Margaret. Art decided he wanted to open his own Juan Pollo and he had a plan. Knowing that Ontario and San Bernardino were the busiest stores he wanted to open halfway between them because he knew it would be surrounded by existing customers.

The city of Fontana fit his requirements. Fontana immediately became the third busiest Juan Pollo. The Ramirez family now operates eight stores.

Sal Ramirez, Art's younger brother saw the success of Fontana and knew he had to open his own store. I first met Sal when he was twelve. He adopted me as his 'father'. He invited himself to go everywhere I went. That included dates with Sella, going out for dinner, visiting friends, and going to the different Juan Pollos.

Sal was a very personable young man with a big smile. The customers always thought Sal was the best worker. In reality Sal did the least amount of work he could because he preferred talking to working. The employees complained about Sal but if he made us look good to the customers that's all that really mattered.

Ramirez Family currently owns and operates 8 Juan Pollo restaurants. (1994)

1997 - Juan Pollo in Perris, California was opened by a friend who owned a Persian restaurant in nearby Corona. She quickly discovered that the Juan Pollo system was not as easy as she thought so she wanted someone to buy her out for the amount of her investment.

Sal and Rocio Ramirez and crew Moreno Valley Restaurant. (1999)

Sal saw an opportunity so he borrowed money from his father-in-law and other relatives to buy the store. Sal worked every day along with his wife Rocio (also a former employee) and his crew leader Rosa. With fast service and emphasis on quality food their sales increased every month allowing them to pay off their loans. In two years they had enough additional savings to open their second store in Moreno Valley, California.

This pattern of allowing former employees to open their own stores continued through the early 2000s. By 2010 there were thirty-two Juan Pollos, twenty-two of which were owned and operated by ex-hourly employees.

Life Lesson Learned:
Building your company from within builds loyalty.

FUTURE JUAN POLLO OWNERS?

29

BOSTON MARKET – BIG PLANS GONE AWRY

Boston Market started in New England in 1985 as Boston Chicken. Steven Kolow and Arthur Cores founded Boston Chicken and had plans to grow huge through franchising.

The plan was to open prototype restaurants selling rotisserie chickens to a new base of health conscious Americans eager to get away from beef products. At the same time the idea called for preparing fresh sides daily in a clean bright atmosphere.

They were very eager to expand so they went public in 1993 and raised millions of dollars. They had dreams of becoming the McDonald's of the chicken business.

After hearing much hype about the Boston Chicken rotisserie concept, Armando and I took a trip to New England to investigate the company. The idea sounded great on paper, but the entire company including the founder, executives, district managers, general managers, and the cooks neglected to learn how to cook chickens that people would be willing to pay money for.

Without a good tasting chicken I knew they were doomed

to mediocrity. In my opinion Boston Chicken was nothing more than a legal pyramid scheme. The owners were in the right place at the right time. The public became infatuated with rotisserie chicken and Boston Market rode that frenzy. Their early income was derived from one-time development fees and royalties. When the company went public the stock prices kept rising because of all the positive publicity. Early investors were getting wealthy from stock price increases but at the store level very few were profitable.

To expand faster Boston Chicken's strategy was to sell area franchises to big investors. When Boston Chicken came to California to scout for locations they picked the prime locations and paid whatever prices landlords asked.

The corporate officials held secret meetings with El Pollo Loco and KFC managers and told them they were going to put their companies out of business so they better join them. A large percentage of these managers and district managers defected. I thought it was hilarious that anyone working at the other chicken chains could view Boston Chicken as a threat to their livelihood just because Boston Chicken told them they were going to open up next to them. I knew that Boston Chicken was in trouble if they hired people dumb enough to believe these wild claims without first checking out their product and business model. It was the blind leading the blind.

When Boston Chicken started opening restaurants in Southern California they had lines of curious customers. Boston Chicken had premium locations, the best equipment, large open dining rooms, and plenty of staffing. The district managers and store managers were greeting everyone at the front door while the teenage minimum wage employees were behind the counter cooking the chickens. I couldn't believe that the corporate philosophy was to put their management as store greeters and have the unskilled employees cooking their chickens. It was no wonder that very few people thought much of their chicken product. The management should have been the ones cooking the chickens and training the hourly employees.

Boston Market didn't talk much about their chicken product because nobody in the company knew how to properly cook rotisserie chickens. Their marinade consisted of injecting the chickens with a salt solution. The chicken procedures seemed secondary. Even the company acknowledged that they were really in the side order business. Boston Chicken took great pride in promoting the fact that all their 'sides' were freshly made in their kitchen and kept fresh by only preparing small batches at a time. If their best feature was fresh side orders, they should have called themselves 'Boston Fresh Sides' instead of Boston Chicken. In 1995 they did change their name to Boston Market so they could sell ham, turkey, and beef products. It seemed that few customers liked their bland chicken.

As Boston Market started opening throughout the country very few were profitable and their debt became unbearable. By 1998 Boston Market filed for Chapter 11 bankruptcy and was purchased by McDonald's Corporation. They bought Boston Market for their prime locations because they wanted to convert them into Chipotle Mexican Grill restaurants. McDonald's got intrigued by the rotisserie chicken business and decided to keep the chain operating even though they had a poor reputation with consumers.

The ironic part of their story is that by the time the company filed bankruptcy their marinade was much improved and their chicken product was quite decent.

Boston Chicken unintentionally created a bonus for Juan Pollo. During their rapid growth the equipment manufacturers were recording record profits from selling high priced rotisserie cookers because the demand was so high. After filing bankruptcy, many of

Early Boston chicken restaurant (1990)

the stores were liquidated at auctions. The cookers that sold new for six thousand dollars were initially selling for one thousand to two thousand dollars. There were so many machines going into the secondary market that cookers eventually sold for as little as three hundred dollars. Boston Chicken liquidated entire stores for pennies on the dollar. We had a field day going to all the auctions and buying high quality equipment at rock bottom prices. There are still hundreds of rotisserie cookers in storage all over the country and because of this the prices should stay low for a long time.

McDonald's eventually sold the Boston Market chain but they are operating as a shadow of what they once were.

Life Lesson Learned:

You can't fool the public with flash and style. If your food doesn't taste good, no one will pay money for it.

30

WAL-MART – "MADE IN AMERICA"

Many people criticize Wal-Mart as the scourge of small business but I view them as one of the very successful stories in American history.

1964 - Sam Walton opened his first Wal-Mart in Bentonville, Arkansas. When he decided to expand every expert in the field said it was too late to compete head to head with established giants such as Sears, K-Mart, and Target. Within fifty years Wal-Mart became the world's largest retailer leaving Sears and K-Mart in shambles.

I am not a retailing expert but when I read *"Made in America"* in 1992, it became clear why Wal-Mart grew so huge and so fast. Sam Walton was a marketing genius who made a personal connection with the American working class and said, "I am one of you, I want to save you money, I support America." He hired retired local citizens and made them official door greeters. He donated money to schools and charities but most of all he had the lowest prices in town.

Wal-Mart also came along when the computer age arrived. Sam Walton used this new technology while the older established

Sam Walton's Book Made in America (1992)

chains were resistant to change. Wal-Mart pioneered computerized inventory and cash control systems. They were able to track deliveries and control their buying so there was a quick turnaround. Lower costs of doing business were passed along to customers as lower prices. In the end Sam Walton gave the American public what it really wanted: a wide selection of goods the lowest prices and old-fashioned friendly service.

When Wal-Mart first came to California in the early 1990s I couldn't wait to see what all the hype was about. Many articles were written in the local newspapers about the coming behemoth and how they would affect the local businesses and economy. Every article also talked about Wal-Mart's low prices so this made the average person want to shop there even more. This amounted to free publicity.

Although Target and K-mart remodeled their stores in anticipation of Wal-Mart's opening they couldn't compete with the

(1962) first Discount store located at 719 Walnut Ave. in Rogers, Arkansas.

lines of customers. I was amazed that although each of the three stores was similar in design and layout and sold the same goods Wal-Mart had the 'buzz' and the others didn't. Sam Walton imparted intangible qualities into the company that made them stand out in the crowd.

I saw the future for my business. What Wal-Mart did in America I need to do overseas. Juan Pollo is still a long way from expanding to China or India but Wal-Mart has provided me with the blueprint for success:

1. Make a personal connection with your customer base.
2. Embrace the local community as your own.
3. Sell the best quality at the lowest prices.
4. Take advantage of new technology before your competition.

Sam Walton was humble and accessible in public yet ferocious and demanding behind the scenes. Sam Walton was an icon.

Life lesson Learned:
You can be a late-comer and still grow huge if you understand the intangible qualities Wal-Mart used to crush the competition.

SUPER DISASTER
SUNDAY JAN 31 1993

DALLAS COWBOYS   **52**

BUFFALO BILLS   **17**

JUAN POLLO   **0**

31

SUPER BOWL XXVII – OUR WORST DAY EVER

1993 - We had mastered large party order sales. Holidays and special event days such as the Superbowl got busier each year because we learned how to handle multiple party orders at the same time. During the early years holidays created problems because we would always run short of chickens. The secret of these busy days was timing. Our motto could easily be 'timing is everything.'

We were expecting a record Superbowl sales day in San Bernardino. The Dallas Cowboys were playing the Buffalo Bills. The Saturday before the game my wife Sella, and I were stocking up for the anticipated crowds. Jose, the original San Bernardino cook who started in 1986 also stayed to help. Sella was busy stocking salsa and preparing potato salad while Jose was marinating extra chickens and getting all the spits ready.

Jose had worked every Superbowl Sunday since we opened and Sella only worked at the San Bernardino location for a couple of years so Jose kept trying to tell Sella how busy it was going to be and she better make sure everything was stocked. Sella told him to mind

Jose Morales cooking chicken for SUPER BOWL Sunday (1993)

his own business and make sure he didn't run out of chickens.

By Saturday night we already had twenty-five large party orders for Sunday. The only way we could handle this was to stockpile cooked chickens in our warmers. If the chickens were cooked properly they would still be a good product after two hours in a warmer. We instructed Jose to start cooking at 5:00 a.m. because we needed fifteen trays of cooked chickens by noon. Everything was set for us to have a record day.

I arrived in San Bernardino about 11:30 a.m. and knew right away we were going to run out of chickens. The machines were half empty and the chickens cooking were very raw. There were about ten trays of cooked chickens but that would only last a couple of hours. I immediately turned the fires to high and demanded Jose load up all

Pancho choping chicken on worst day ever (1993)

the spits and put them in the machines.

I was angry at Jose because he knew better. I realized he had to be 'high' on marijuana because he looked confused, didn't have any idea what time it was, and had a history of recreational use. His thinking was clouded so he thought he had too many chickens but in reality he was setting us up for the worst day in our history.

Although I knew we were doomed I had no idea how bad it would get. By 12:30 p.m. we were cooking to order and we still had all of our party orders to fill. There was a line of walk-in customers and they were all ordering multiple orders of chickens. We were also getting last minute phone orders.

By 1:00p.m. the lines kept getting longer not shorter. The line out the door reached over one hundred feet. There was at least an hour wait. The dining room was full of anxious customers impatiently waiting for their orders. The order wheel was completely filled with tickets. We started taping the extra tickets all over the front counters.

Sella was in charge of sorting out the orders when chickens were ready. As the customers with phone orders started coming in they bypassed the lines and went straight to Sella expecting to pick up their chickens. If we gave them the fresh chickens the other customers started complaining they were there first. Whatever she did half of the customers ended up angry.

Jose's brother Pancho was cutting the chickens and putting them in the containers. He started telling some of the mexican customers to come back in an hour and he would have chicken for them. I didn't know what he was saying because he was speaking Spanish. When these people came back the wait was even longer but they demanded the chickens Pancho promised them. We had nothing to give them.

By 2:00 p.m. it was a complete disaster. We had order tickets taped all over the front counter. Customers were waiting over an hour and a half. The customers were going to miss the opening kick-off. The line out the door was now about two hundred feet towards the next building.

Everyone was angry. Many wanted refunds. The phone order people were angry because they placed their orders early and many had paid in advance. The customers who walked in without pre-ordering were angry because others got their orders before they did. The people Pancho told to come back were angry because they thought they had a deal. Most of the others took their anger out on my wife who happened to be six months pregnant with our first baby. Finally we filled all the orders. At our peak disaster point we were over one hundred and fifty chickens behind. We have never had a worse day in our history. This whole nightmare never should have occurred.

By the way, the game was a rout by the Cowboys, 52-17.

Life Lesson Learned:
No matter how much preparation you put into something execution and timing are everything.

32

'SITE OF THE ORIGINAL McDONALD'S' FOR SALE

1998 - Juan Pollo kept me so busy I rarely had time to read the daily newspaper. One June Sunday I happened to buy the *San Bernardino Sun* and discovered that the site of the original McDonald's was in foreclosure and no one wanted it. It had experienced many failed escrows.

Although the original restaurant was demolished in 1972 the property included a refurbished 4,000 square foot commercial building and the remnants of the original golden arches street sign. At one hundred and thirty-five thousand dollars I knew I had to buy the property. The following Monday I called a realtor friend and made an offer to buy. I didn't really know what I would do with the building but I sensed that I would get much free press and the publicity alone would be worth the price.

The day I closed escrow there were two articles in the *San Bernardino Sun* and a front page story in the *Riverside Press Enterprise* telling of the purchase of the site. KNX "all news" radio in Los Angeles mentioned the purchase every hour.

ORIGINAL McDONALD'S 14th and E Street San Bernardino, California (1954)

One of the newspaper columns said I was going to open a McDonald's Museum. I decided to move our corporate offices into the building and at the same time take the newspapers' idea to open an unofficial McDonald's Museum.

I called the three local McDonald's franchisees and asked them to help me start my museum but they were afraid the corporation would forbid them. I tried to tell them they would be known all over the McDonald's empire as the ones who saved the original site but they didn't share that vision. They were more interested is keeping peace with the corporation so they wouldn't jeopardize future profits.

I realized that no one was going to help with my museum so I started doing research on the early history of McDonald's. The first thing I learned was two brothers Dick and Mac opened McDonald's Bar-B-Que in 1940 serving a wide variety of food items. They had car hops serving the customers and within a few years they became the most popular teen hang out in San Bernardino. With the success of the restaurant the brothers became two of the wealthiest men in

McDONALD'S Corporation officially designates property as
"HISTORIC SITE OF THE ORIGINAL McDONALD'S (1992)

the county. Although they had more money than they imagined they could earn the brothers became disenchanted with extensive food preparation and the lack of customer turnover because the boys would come to socialize with the carhops. Dick realized that eighty per cent of their sales were hamburgers and French fries. He also realized there was going to be a booming family trade business soon because World War II just ended and everyone was eager to raise families.

1948 - They closed the restaurant, revamped their kitchen, and reopened on December 12 as McDonald's Hamburgers. Inspired by Henry Ford and the Ford Motor company they introduced the 'Speedee' service system which revolutionized the hamburger business by using mass production techniques to lower prices and provide consistency of every burger served. After a slow start business exceeded their wildest expectations and the rest is history.

I closed escrow in August 1998 and after receiving little help

from McDonald's franchisees. I started making plans for my unofficial museum. By October someone mentioned that December 12 would be McDonald's fifty-year anniversary! I immediately called the mayor's office and told her we were going to have our grand opening of the unofficial McDonald's Museum on the actual fifty-year anniversary. She didn't think we could pull it off because the building was completely empty and we only had two months to get ready.

I put everyone to work and we pulled off our grand opening on December 12, 1998 the official 50 year anniversary date. Since then there have been hundreds of visitors from all over the world visiting the museum. Many have brought their memorabilia to put on display so they can share it with others. We have collected stories and experiences from previous employees and customers.

Grand opening of the "HISTORIC SITE OF THE ORIGINAL McDONALD'S" museum. Mayor Judith Valles celebrates 50th year anniversary of first McDonald's. (Dec 12-1998)

Free Admission open 10-5 daily. Museum specializing in early history of McDonald's.

Albert is proud of the fact that he helped save a piece Route 66 and fast food history. (2000)

As our company grows, we will be known as the company trying to preserve fast food history and we will always be linked to McDonald's.

It has to be destiny that I grew up idolizing McDonald's, watched them become the largest restaurant chain in the world, and ended up owning the site where it all started.

Life Lesson Learned:
Marketing opportunities are always available but you need to recognize them and take action.

33

JUAN POLLO CATERING -'THE KEY TO PROFITS'

Juan Pollo has built its reputation on the quality of its rotisserie chicken but the key to financial success is through catering. Juan Pollo chicken is a perfect food for catering because it holds up well after cooking. Slow cooking allows more of the natural juices to stay in the meat resulting in a tender product that does not require additional sauces. By comparison char-broiled chicken such as El Pollo Loco needs to be eaten shortly after cooking because the longer it sits the 'tougher' the meat becomes. The same could be said about pizza and fried chicken. Other products such as hamburgers must be eaten immediately.

Juan Pollo meals fit in well with almost any budget or event. Rotisserie chicken goes well with weddings, birthday parties, office parties, business lunches, reunions, picnics, funerals, Christmas Eve. New Year's, Mother's Day, Easter, Fourth of July parties, Pay Per View boxing, Superbowls, graduation parties, fundraisers, and any other event where people gather.

Anaheim, California Food Tasting event (2003)

I discovered the connection of catering and profitability in the 1980s. I was working the front counter everyday monitoring the sales and the customers. Whenever someone made a large order of multiple chickens I made sure everything was perfect because I knew they were feeding more than one family. I realized two things would occur if everything went well. The first was if everyone raved about our chicken the person who brought it would keep taking Juan Pollo to his parties. The second thing would be new customers who would seek us out to serve Juan Pollo at their events. Each catering event that went well produced new customers and word of mouth positive reviews.

Over the years we have perfected the art of catering extra large party orders. We have served as many as five thousand guests at one time. Juan Pollo chicken is in demand by many groups because of the health benefits of chicken. The day to day customers pay the bills and the catering orders provide the profits.

Life Lesson Learned:
Catering orders not only improve the bottom line, they greatly increase the Juan Pollo customer base.

34

MILLION-DOLLAR LAWSUIT

2001 - Three disgruntled employees seeking one million dollars in emotional damages sued me. They worked at the San Bernardino location and quit because I supposedly yelled at them for no reason. They went to the labor board and were told that California labor laws would only protect them if sexual harassment or racial discrimination had occurred.

The three disgruntled employees then claimed I used racial epithets on a daily basis apparently forgetting that ninety per cent of all employees were Hispanic and this was the first time an employee claimed racial discrimination.

I felt this lawsuit would benefit me because I had never been sued in civil court and I knew I could gain valuable experience about courtrooms and defending lawsuits. I hired an attorney to defend the lawsuit. As I read their complaints it was obvious that others were coaching them in their written statements. I could not recall any of their specific complaints because they didn't list any. Everything was written in nonspecific terms such as "He called everyone a _ _ _ _-_ _ _ _ every day."

I told my attorney that this was a frivolous lawsuit and I wanted to fight it all the way. When depositions were scheduled, I wanted to be present so I could listen to our questions and their answers. One of the three plaintiffs was a crew leader who spoke perfect English. Amazingly, by the time she was deposed, she apparently forgot she knew English and spoke only Spanish through an interpreter.

Two weeks later, I was scheduled to be deposed by the plaintiff's attorneys. I had prepared for the deposition by providing myself notes that I felt would benefit my case such as a record of all the employees I have helped and their status with Juan Pollo.

Some of the early questions involved the structure of Juan Pollo and the racial make-up of key personnel. They were attempting to show that I operated a two tier-system where family members controlled the money and the Hispanic employees were being exploited for my profit. Before being asked, I explained that I was not operating a family business and the key personnel in the company were Hispanic. Since that avenue of questioning was going nowhere, they turned their questions to the ownership of the various Juan Pollos. I stated that most of the Juan Pollo's were owned and operated by my former employees.

When they asked me how many of these people were Hispanic, I replied that all of them were. I could tell by their facial expressions they didn't expect that answer. At this point, the attorneys requested a short break, left the room, came back and told me there were no further questions

A few weeks later, my attorney called and said he had good news for me. The three girls would drop the lawsuit for $10,000. He said he felt sorry for the other attorneys because at that settlement price, they would not cover their expenses. I told him I could care less about the other attorneys if they were dumb enough to take this lawsuit without investigating the complaint first. Knowing I was innocent of racial discrimination I didn't feel I should pay any money even if they went from one million dollars to ten thousand dollars.

About this time I received a letter from a different attorney saying he was representing Robert Komatsu and was requesting financial information from us. At this point I knew I had to settle the discrimination lawsuit quick because the lawsuit I feared had arrived. I had been preparing ten years for possible legal action from Robert. It had been my hope that Robert would come to me and tell me he wanted to be bought out and give me a price. I knew it wouldn't be that easy. Robert's attorney ignored the fact that financial information was always available because we used his bookkeepers. His lawyers quickly sued claiming money conversion, embezzlement, and unreasonable inflated salaries.

Richard Dietz, a friend from high school volunteered to help me with strategy. Since Robert's attorney made some outrageous charges Richard's strategy was to have our lawyer claim that we were never partners and that the original financial arrangement was just a loan. This infuriated Robert's dad because he felt I betrayed him. I wanted to be able to tell George that the claim was just a part of my defense strategy. Richard's strategy threw off Robert's attorney for a while. The lawyers spent much time going back and forth debating the merits of our claims. As we started going to court for preliminary proceedings, it became apparent that our lawyer was not an experienced courtroom attorney. Although he was a highly educated Harvard graduate, the other attorney was out maneuvering him.

My attorney spent most of his time in front of the judge protesting 'unethical' tactics used by the other attorney rather than concentrating on our motions to get the lawsuit dismissed. It was also apparent to me that the judge knew that we should be settling the case on our own and there was really no need to go to trial. He kept steering the attorneys towards working it out through arbitration. Paperwork was going back and forth between attorneys. Robert's attorney wasn't sure what we were up to and Robert apparently didn't think things were going quick enough so he hired a second attorney to assist in the case.

Robert was smart about strategy. He had the deep pockets to force me into bankruptcy. I think he was more interested in punishing me for being confident and cocky rather than receiving a settlement. I didn't have huge reserves and was barely hanging on. My strategy was to make Robert think I was unpredictable and would go down fighting before giving up. In reality I was anxious for a settlement. Depositions were scheduled and Robert went first. His lawyer was very skilled at intercepting every question rephrasing it so it only required a yes or no answer. When Robert was finished my attorney subpoenaed George Komatsu for deposition. I knew this was the last thing George wanted because this was a matter between Robert and myself. I felt bad that George would have to go through this but Robert's lawsuit forced me.

Before my deposition another friend from high school Eugene Hayashibara, told me one of his dental clients was a partnership and business attorney who volunteered to take a look at the lawsuit. He stated I was fortunate Robert's attorney didn't specialize in business litigation because Robert was legally entitled to fifty percent of everything. After hearing his opinion I was nervous about preceeding to trial.

Robert's attorney was very skilled at interrogation. At my deposition he made everything seem like an attempt to deceive and embezzle money from Robert. He told me he was prepared to go over every financial paper he had subpoenaed which led me to believe he was more interested in padding his bill.

Before the second day of my deposition I received an unexpected call from Robert. He told me he had breakfast with his father and they discussed the case. Right away I knew the case was over! I am sure that George was tired of the whole affair and told Robert he should settle.

Robert told me that he wanted one million dollars and not a penny less. I quickly agreed. He also told me that I had to pay for his attorney's fees and I agreed. In retrospect I shouldn't have agreed so fast to pay his attorney's fees because they amounted to over two hundred thousand dollars.

I felt that I would one day recover the million dollars by writing a book about my struggles to build a rotisserie chicken chain when everyone else failed. People want to read about becoming successful through hard work perseverance and positive thinking. Nobody wants to read a book about becoming wealthy when everything was handed to you.

Life Lesson Learned:
Overcoming adversity will make you stronger.

Albert with the JUAN POLLO 1988 Toyota 4X4 Monster Truck. (1996)

35

JUAN POLLO MARKETING

1990 - A Jack Marcus came to the San Bernardino store and told me he wanted to make us a series of Juan Pollo Pogs. I had no idea who Jack was or what a Pog was. I asked him repeatedly why I should do business with him.

Jack told me that these odd sounding things were liners in bottle caps. These bottle caps became collectibles in Hawaii when bottlers started putting designs and characters on these liners. The actual name 'Pog' stood for a brand of juice made from passionfruit, orange, and guava. Jack said that Pogs would become the new craze in California. He was right. Soon everyone was playing with Pogs. Jack designed a series of Juan Pollo Pogs using cartoon characters he invented. With the success of the Pogs I was able to put Jack on the payroll as our marketing director. Jack stayed with us for the next twenty years.

After the Pog craze died down, the Power Rangers, a series about teenage superheroes became the rage with pre-teens. Jack

Jack Marcus graphic designer and cartoonist. (2002)

developed Juan Pollo's version of chicken crime fighters, the 'Power Pollo Rangers'.

The late 1990s brought the Pokemon phenomenon that started with the cartoon characters from Japan and turned into a tremendously successful card game. Jack drew a variety of 'Polloman' cartoon characters, each with their own powers and rankings. He came up with his own card game using his new characters.

Jack got us into the newspaper loop. He would call newspapers and give press releases about promotional work he was doing. Jack would talk them into additional articles about the restaurants. Jack became very adept at 'embellishing' small articles or mentions in the papers and turning them into impressive looking stories.

Every year the local newspaper would call me to find out what our new promotion would be.

Other newspapers would search me out to write articles about the business. They would call for opinions on topics such as minimum wages, the effect of economy on business, inflation, food price increases, or information about the company's growth plans.

1990s - JM Productions designed these promotional items for Juan Pollo.

First Juan Pollo Parade 5th Street and Mt Vernon Ave San Bernardino, California Cinco de Mayo 1986

Albert and Sella Okura at Black History Parade Riverside, California (2002)

1993 Caddillac boat named the "SS Juan Pollo" originally owned by comedian Gallagher.

Whenever I talk to reporters I make sure I keep talking and throw out many ideas, plans, or theories and most of all, never be boring or predictable. Reporters need to write and editors need to edit. The bigger the article starts off the longer it will end up in print. You need to be readily available to news reporters because if you hesitate they have to move on due to their deadlines. I also realized that you can't believe everything you read in the newspapers because reporters can only write what is told to them and they can't research every fact.

Having a variety of news articles posted in the restaurants presents us as a larger more successful company than we are. I have discovered that perception is reality. If people see us as a large company that's all that matters.

1986 - We participated in our first parade. It consisted of us putting a sign in the back of our work truck and renting a cheap chicken suit. Since that time, we have participated in numerous parades every year.

Juan Pollo attends 10-20 parades every year.

Parades are a tremendous advertising vehicle if you analyze the dynamics of parades. The typical parade participant goes to the parade, sets up, participates in the parade, and then goes home with the same people watching them every year. There can be much more to parades than just participating.

When we attend parades all of our vehicles are parade ready with graphics, characters on top of the cars, flashing lights, and exterior loudspeakers playing theme or seasonal music. We make it a point to caravan from our offices to our destination in full parade mode with flashing lights and music. Many more people see us cruising down the highway than see us in the parades.

Law enforcement is always supportive of us as we slowly make our way through each city. We end up creating our own private parades. If I know the parade route I try to enter the lineup by traveling from the end of the parade to the beginning. That way we get double exposure with the early bird spectators.

Once we are in the parade I try to choreograph the spacing between the vehicles so the spectators have time to see each one pass by as though they were independent entries. We prefer to be at the end of the parade lineup because the "best should be saved for last."

In the early 2000s, I had the opportunity to buy a series of used eight foot tall Warner Brothers cartoon characters that decorated their mall stores. The prices ranged from one thousand to fifteen hundred dollars each. Although I didn't have any use for Daffy Duck, Sylvester, Bugs Bunny, or the Tasmanian Devil, I couldn't resist the once in a lifetime opportunity to own licensed cartoon characters.

I bought all four, took them to my house, and put them in my backyard. They sat there for over one year and the only ones who saw them were relatives or next-door neighbors. For a while I thought I owned four 'white elephants'. One day I put 'Taz' on the bed of one of our parade and car show vehicles. Although the 1966 Ford Ranchero was restored and was painted with our logos and characters the only ones who seemed to notice were car enthusiasts.

Putting 'Taz' on the car was like night and day. All of a sudden everyone noticed the car. People would honk, mothers would point us out to their kids, teens would laugh, toddlers would wave, and everyone with a camera phone would take pictures.

Juan Pollo dummy poses by 1966 Ford Ranchero with "Taz" as passanger (2001)

Soon I mounted the characters on our other parade vehicles. Warner Brothers Cartoon characters have timeless appeal to people of all ages. 'Taz' is probably more popular today than when I was a child.

Official 2001 Chevrolet parade truck with Daffy Duck.

Each of the vehicles has exterior speakers to play appropriate music. The songs attract attention the cartoon characters cause people to do a 'double take' and everyone sees the Juan Pollo name on the vehicles.

Life Lesson Learned;
If you want to get the maximum publicity for the least amount of effort and money you need to do things that make you stand out in a crowd.

36

TOWN FOR SALE

Route 66 was established by the United States Government in 1926 as the first continuous road system connecting California to Chicago. For many years Route 66 was the main entry way into Southern California from the East.

As a result hundreds of businesses sprung up along the route catering to thousands of travelers seeking their fortunes on the West Coast. By the 1970s freeways and interstates were being built at record pace and Route 66 fell by the wayside.

This led to many closed businesses and abandoned towns. One such town along the route was Amboy, California. Founded in the 1800s, Amboy was a bustling town located in the Mojave Desert halfway between Barstow and Needles. Interstate 40 opened in 1972 and almost overnight Amboy's business dried up. Eventually Amboy was a virtual ghost town consisting of a post office, gas station, school, café, and iconic thirty-five foot Roy's Café sign.

1998 - Buster Burris, longtime owner of Amboy and his wife Bessie retired to nearby Wonder Valley and sold the entire town to Walt Wilson and his friend Tim White.

Roy's Motel Cafe sign is one of the most photographed signs on Historical Route 66.

This view shows Roy's Gas Station, Roy's Cafe, Motel Lobby, 2 of the 6 Bungalow Cabins, Radio Tower, Water Towers and Roy's Sign. (2009)

In 2003, E-Bay was just begining to flex it's muscles on the internet. E-Bay received world wide publicity by putting three towns for sale on their website. Walt and Tim put Amboy for sale as the third town. My friend and Route 66 expert Danny Castro, called me and told me I needed to buy the town because it would compliment the Site of the Original McDonald's museum. Although I am a native Californian, I had never heard of Amboy. I asked Danny what Amboy was and he told me it was the most valuable Route 66 attraction in California and in danger of being lost due to neglect.

Amboy Cemetary established in 1861. (2008)

Bungalow Cabins were built in 1947. (2008)

We took a three hour drive to Amboy to see first hand what was for sale at the asking price of 1.2 million dollars. After we took a tour of the town from Walt Wilson I knew I had to buy this famous town. I thought about my friend Ray Millman and his regrets about not owning his own town.

I negotiated a tentative deal with Walt and Tim. While working out terms of the purchase the deal fell through because the Internal Revenue Service informed me that our corporate tax returns for Juan Pollo had not been filed for prior years. It took two years and much money to resolve the problem.

During this time real estate values in Southern California

St. Raymond's Church built in 1951. (2009)

According to *"Silence and the Sun"* this church mural was painted by Patrick Fahey.

skyrocketing. I would never be able to afford owning my own town if prices kept rising.

On Good Friday 2005, my office received an urgent e-mail from Bob Lundy, President of San Bernardino County Tourism. He forwarded an e-mail from Bonnie Barnes who stated that Amboy was going to be sold at noon for $770,000 cash or best offer. I didn't know who Bonnie was or what was going on with Amboy.

Bessie Burris had repossessed Amboy from Walt and Tim. She was heartbroken that Amboy was allowed to deteriorate from its former glory. Bonnie was Bessie's grand daughter and she was help-ing Bessie find the right buyer. They wanted someone who would honor the town's historic past.

Closing of Amboy sale was front page news San Bernardino Sun 4/13/2005

When I got in touch with Bonnie I told her of my interest in preserving Amboy plus my efforts to preserve the history of the original McDonald's. I told Bonnie I would be glad to pay the money she wanted but I would need time to arrange financing. Bonnie replied she was going to sell Amboy for the best cash offer because she didn't want to carry papers. I asked what the best offer was and she told me $375,000.

I told her I would pay $400,000. Bonnie told me she would think about it and let me know Saturday. The next day Bonnie called and asked me a few more questions about my sincerity in restoring Amboy. She then told me she had a better offer but if we would pay $425,000 cash and come sign papers that night, we would have a deal, I agreed.

Miss Amboy 2009 Nina De Carlo and admirer.

This Amboy Post Office location has been in continous operation since 1951 (2008)

I met with Bonnie and Bessie that night and I promised Bessie I would do my best to honor her family memory in Amboy. We closed escrow and I ended up owning a famous town.

The town is not yet a fully functioning town but the post office, gas station, and twenty-four hour restrooms are open to the public. Amboy is a town where time has stood still since the 1960's. The world wide internet has allowed instant access to information. People all over the world have become interested in discovering the true histories of events and places such as Route 66 and Amboy. Amboy is a stepping stone for worldwide recognition for Juan Pollo.

Life Lesson Learned:
Being in the right place at right time to buy a famous town had to be destiny.

37

JUAN POLLO AND MONOPOLY

The decade of the 2000s proved to be tumultuous, exciting, disappointing, and eye opening. Tumultuous describes the lawsuit that could have broken up the company. The lawsuit years proved very stressful with much uncertainty about our future. The company survived but the war chest was depleted of funds.

2005 - The opportunity arose to buy Amboy. Believing it was destiny to own a historical town that would always be famous world-wide I extended every line of credit to complete the deal. Although Amboy has been a drain on the finances to date the investment will return a hundred fold when all is said and done. The value is the branding of Juan Pollo as keeper of the town. Route 66 is becoming a cultural phenomenon that is predicted to grow rapidly every year.

The newer stores that opened in the 2000s have under performed in terms of potential. One of the reasons is the owners have not learned the correct cooking proceedures that lead to high volume. This along with the nation wide recession has created a drain on cash flow.

Although there are many restaurants and grocery stores that sell rotisserie chicken there is no rotisserie chicken restaurant chain that has potential to grow except Juan Pollo.

Although it has been somewhat disappointing that the original owners have not trained, developed, or motivated their crew leaders and management as I hoped I can't expect others to share my drive and ambition. That doesn't stop me from trying to instill these traits with everyone I meet.

The 2000s have had ups and downs but has produced one eye opening fact that outweighs everything to date: Juan Pollo has ended up with a monopoly! After all these years there is no competition from any rotisserie chicken chain. Everyone who has attempted to create a rotisserie chain has failed. The list includes Boston Market, Kenny Rodgers, KFC Rotisserie Gold, Koo Koo Roo's, and countless other startups.

There are some rotisserie chicken restaurants but most are copycats of Juan Pollo that resemble 'mom and pop' operations or small chains such as Armenian style Zankou chicken which is too ethnic to become a mainstream chain.

The idea of selling a universal food such as rotisserie chicken sounds very simple but few have become successful in mass producing rotisserie chickens because the art of cooking chickens is much more difficult than it appears. There have been countless numbers of Juan Pollo copycats that have opened and failed. The most common reason for failure was the owners believing customers would buy their chickens because of the style of cooking not the quality or flavor of the chickens. None of these copycats have taken the time to learn the chicken cooking skills I talk about over and over in this book.

Official JUAN POLLO logo and chicken character trademarked in 1986.

Juan Pollo will always have a monopoly on rotisserie chickens because if anyone rises up that can present a challenge to us I will let them join us instead of having to compete with us. Juan Pollo has two qualities that no new company can overcome unless we falter. The first is reputation and the second is the time we have been open. You cannot buy either of these two attributes with any amount of money. Juan Pollo has built its reputation over a span of almost three decades.

Life Lesson Learned:

If you create a company that ends up as a monopoly the key is to recognize it and take advantage.

OKURA FAMILY Chino, California location. (2012)

38

OKURA FAMILY TREE

Since my ancestors originally emigrated from Asia, many casual observers assume that I operate as a family buiness. All of my grandparents came to America in the 1910s and I spent my whole life here so the only thing I know about Asian countries is they are proud people and they don't like each other.

I have tried to pattern Juan Pollo after the Japanese business model. World War II left Japan in tatters and their economy was almost non-existent. The surviving companies relied on teamwork, motivation, hard work, in-house promotions, and life time employment for a loyal workforce. When mid-level managers were promoted to positions beyond their ability, they were allowed to transfer to jobs better suited for their skills. Companies had a genuine interest in the welfare of their employees and for fifty years Japan prospered with this system.

My actual family started about ten years into Juan Pollo. I was so busy in the early years I didn't have time to think about finding a spouse or raise a family.

Okura Family (2003)

Armando thought it was time I got married so he suggested his sister-in-law Gisella Oei, start working for me at the San Bernardino location. I first met Sella while working at Del Taco but at the time I didn't know Sella possessed natural management abilities. Had I known we would have gotten married much earlier. When I tell friends that I only married Sella because she was a good manager she gives me a funny look because she knows I'm not really joking.

Kyle Lee was born in 1993. I would have preferred Kyle going to work with me when he was young, Sella and her family wouldn't allow it. At age fifteen I told Kyle he was old enough to work one day a week. Kyle and his younger brother Aaron did work but spent most of the time relaxing and eating. I told Sella our kids were lazy and she let me know my opinions weren't appreciated.

Saiid demonstrating the art of cooking chicken to Kyle and Aaron Okura. (1999)

The following summer I told the boys we were trying it again. This time I told Kyle that he had to cook the chickens. Rather than complain Kyle took a proactive approach to cooking. Instead of waiting for me to explain the details of cooking, he jumped in and started cooking. He would look at the chickens and start telling me which ones were done and why.

This was the first time anyone started explaining what he was doing before training started. Without instruction Kyle was trying to cook every chicken perfect. He took pride showing me his finished products and was able to accurately critique each chicken for its quality. Unlike new cooks who unwittingly manhandle cooked chickens as they take them of the spits Kyle treated each chicken as a valuable and fragile commodity. His actions seem so simple yet no one I had trained approached cooking in this manner.

Kyle has a natural concern for others. Kyle wanted every chicken cooked just right for every customer. He stayed with the machines all day and always knew when it was time to take the chickens out. He did this whether I was present or not. Kyle reinforced my belief that age, education, intelligence, work experience, or even hard work is not the main ingredient for the business. Success requires a natural concern for others. I can recognize this quality but cannot teach it. Everyone claims to have a concern for others but few have demonstrated it through their actions.

In his personal life Kyle has many friends and is generally the one leading his group. His confident 'attitude' that borders on arrogance can be a blessing or a curse. Few people can achieve true success without drive or attitude to propel them forward but if pointed in the wrong direction these traits can lead to mediocrity or despair. Kyle has the intangible qualities to run a major company. My hope is that he recognizes his strengths and has the desire to lead Juan Pollo into the big time.

Aaron Lee was born in 1994. My first impression of Aaron was that he was the most perfectly formed baby I had ever seen. By comparison Kyle resembled an alien for his first few days. Aaron was such a 'cute' baby that my sister-in-law practically adopted Aaron. Growing up I rarely saw Aaron because he always seemed to be at 'Joan's house'. In spite of this I can identify with Aaron and see many parallels in our lives.

We both were second born. Each of our older brothers was more athletic, made friends easier, and showed more leadership during youth. Aaron and I were better students and received better

Aaron at his 5th grade show and tell Grandparents Day demonstrating his plans for the future. (2006)

grades even though intelligence was about equal.

During middle school and high school I was content to be a follower. I grew into leadership roles as I matured. I see Aaron as a late bloomer because he also prefers to follow even though he possesses natural leadership qualities.

I would have preferred to have Aaron helping me when he was ten years old but 'Oma' (grandma) didn't think it was a good idea. I had to wait until he was fourteen but by that age he was not used to working so it was a chore to get Aaron and Kyle out of the house in the morning.

That first year of work was more like a year of play. It ended up a year of learning how to work.

The second year Aaron took the job more seriously and proved to be a very conscientious employee. Although Aaron didn't do the cooking he was doing everything necessary to get the orders out.

I believe Aaron's future is to oversee Juan Pollo operations overseas most likely China. The reason I say this is a religious seer from Indonesia predicted it. Sella's family immigrated to America from Indonesia during the 1980s. Although her family was Chinese descent and not native Indonesian they have adopted some of the local beliefs.

Every two years her family gathers to listen to a religious medium they believe is able to predict the future. I have never been to these readings but the family has told me that he is always accurate. The seer gave his reading in Chinese so it needed to be interpreted into English as he spoke.

He predicted that Aaron was going far away at some point in his life. Aaron is not quite sure what was said and doesn't relish the idea of moving to a foreign country but I seen it as an omen. Aaron has to be headed to China most likely to oversee Juan Pollo franchising. I believe Aaron has a destiny and he will discover it.

In the past I was not sure who or what to believe because every one is constantly bombarded with predictions from horoscopes, handwriting analysis, palm reading, tarot cards, astrology, etc. I realized there is a simple way to handle these predictions. If the message is something positive and good; believe it is true. If the message is something negative or bad you need to believe it is false and hogwash. Embrace good news and reject bad news because whatever you believe will come true.

Chloe Lee was born in 1997. Business wise I am fortunate to have two sons but I always wanted a daughter of my own. Unfortunately Sella wanted a daughter even more. She cried for joy when

Chloe and Sella celebrating Albert's birthday. (2007)

Chloe was born and they have been inseparable ever since.

Besides being a gifted singer, a natural actress, a dancer, artist, and of course an 'A' student, Chloe has shown natural leadership ability and business sense.

For example all through early school years Chloe would be the first student to raise her hand with questions or answers. Chloe answered questions in complete sentences and would add additional information as needed. She would always volunteer to help others, take the time to explain problems clearly, and carefully go over answers as though she was the teacher.

When the children were young Sella would take them to Denny's for breakfast. I came home one day and noticed Chloe had drawn pictures of food on papers that were folded in half. There were pictures of eggs, pancakes, milk, etc. all arranged in the same order. There was no writing because Chloe was too young to read or write. I asked what these were and she replied they were menus. Instead of making one menu as most children would Chloe made multiple menus similar to what you would find in an actual restaurant serving multiple customers.

One day Chloe asked me if I thought ten dollars was a good number. I asked her what she meant. She said that when we open restaurants in China we should have a ten dollar deal. She is right. The Chinese believe in lucky numbers. I think ten is a good number even in America. Chloe was talking price points as a child.

When Chloe was about eleven years old she told me the quality she admired the most about me was that I was always the same. At home she never saw me get angry or raise my voice as some parents do. Since Chloe never came to work I was concerned that Chloe might see me 'yelling' at one of the cooks or scolding an employee with harsh language thus ruining her perception of me.

I started to explain that if she ever saw me get angry with a worker there was a reason. As soon as I brought the subject up she interrupted me and said that when she gets older she would go to the store and train the workers the proper way. Once they were trained she said she would go to the next store and train the workers. Finally, she said that if the first store slacked off she would go back and retrain them. I was worried about disappointing Chloe but she turned it around and ended up explaining the basic theory of upper management. From birth Chloe's thought process is that of an executive not an average person. She will end up running the company. She knows it and I know it.

39

2012 AND BEYOND

By 2011, there were thirty-two Juan Pollos. The company operated as a loose knit organization not a professional corporation and not a family operated business.

2011 was a bad year financially for California businesses and it was worse for the State of California. Operating with enormous budget deficits the state created agencies to collect additional revenue from companies with multiple units which could be operating in violation of franchising laws. Although Juan Pollo was a borderline case. The threat of fines and penalties made the company take steps to comply with the franchise tax laws.

In 2012, Juan Pollo became a legal franchising company. Legally having the right to sell franchises and actually having successful franchisees are two different things. The current corporate structure lacks the key personnel needed to train, develop, and oversee a franchising program. Many restaurants overextended their systems through franchising and many ended in bankruptcy.

Juan Pollo is a vehicle for growth that has been gaining momentum every year. It has become bigger than any one person. Every

Juan Pollo family dolls by Jack Marcus Productions.

great 'break through' company has two qualities that sets them apart from others. The first is a business model that will appeal to the masses. The second is a founder or visionary who becomes the driving force behind the company and is willing to sacrifice everything to achieve sucess. I am that person.

This book has been written in the hopes the right people will read these stories and be inspired to open their own business or be inspired to join Juan Pollo . . .

40

EPILOGUE: FOUR STEPS FOR JUAN POLLO SUCCESS

In order for Juan Pollo to reach its potential, four things need to be accomplished.

1. Juan Pollo needs to become a strong regional chain maintaining our mission statement of "Selling the best tasting rotisserie chicken at the best prices". Prototypes need to be developed for future markets. With streamlined operations we can jump overseas. In this era of instant communications and instant notoriety it is not necessary to be a major chain to be successful in foreign markets.

2. Technology needs to re-invent methods of processing the raw chickens. We need a 'quick frozen', fully marinated, bacteria free chicken that can be put directly into rotisserie cookers. Fresh 'ice pack' chickens present too many potential problems with spoilage or diseases such as salmonella.

3. The current rotisserie cookers are antiquated and labor intensive. Fully automated computer controlled rotisserie ovens need to be invented to fit our specific needs and cook the same quality chicken.

4. The economic giants of this century will probably be China and India. A small company cannot become successful in foreign markets because they will get lost in the shuffle unless they possess intangible qualities such as having a 'celebrity' owner/founder. Marketing yourself as the savior of Route 66 Amboy and savior of the 'Historic Site' of the Original McDonalds can provide the recognition needed.

The following two pages are the actual sales history of the Ontario and San Bernardino locations from Jan 1984 - Aug 1993 as typed by Albert for his promotional sales books: ------------>

Pencil sketch of Flagship Juan Pollo location by Route 66 Illustrator - Robert Waldmire. (2008)
1945-2009

Visit our Flagship Restaurant Location 1258 W. 5th St.
San Bernardino, California 92411

JUAN POLLO #1
ONTARIO SALES HISTORY

	1984	1985	1986	1987	1988
Jan.	4,269	17,219	34,000	59,782	84,370
Feb.	19,184	18,436	30,127	61,324	74,298
March	18,814	24,000	38,355	70,345	76,091
April	15,700	28,200	40,786	69,426	76,500
May	20,512	29,971	45,477	79,274	89,090
June	17,950	30,271	47,304	73,839	90,848
July	19,700	30,056	48,368	80,833	95,509
Aug.	18,688	30,675	51,390	84,655	84,146
Sept.	19,260	30,600	51,564	75,766	81,403
Oct.	18,948	32,000	55,886	79,196	84,223
Nov.	17,087	33,460	60,000	75,697	72,318
Dec.	16,603	31,400	59,400	87,462	82,200
Totals	206,715	336,288	562,847	897,597	990,996
		+63%	+67%	+59%	+10%

	1989	1990	1991	1992	1993
Jan.	75,533	84,538	81,642	92,284	96,971
Feb.	76,026	81,132	79,960	97,705	101,429
March	84,911	92,851	96,981	103,424	108,018
April	90,985	92,088	96,693	99,905	116,337
May	88,322	93,905	102,587	110,253	127,303
June	86,695	96,920	101,739	108,650	115,485
July	93,743	96,867	100,210	115,481	122,427
Aug.	87,802	91,253	100,180	112,088	123,835
Sept.	85,714	89,205	97,999	101,114	
Oct.	82,235	88,442	95,328	111,221	
Nov.	81,635	84,048	91,221	96,597	
Dec.	92,464	93,039	96,557	103,529	
Total	1,026,065	1,084,288	1,141,097	1,252,25	
	+4%	+6%	+5%	+9%	

JUAN POLLO #2
SAN BERNARDINO SALES HISTORY

	1986	1987	1988	1989
Jan.	17,199	35,458	60,917	64,413
Feb.	24,175	36,956	57,655	62,011
March	21,419	40,940	56,638	74,223
April	19,207	39,678	58,540	78,005
May	20,700	44,846	60,800	81,380
June	19,207	43,312	66,125	80,086
July	19,361	46,300	77,272	79,678
Aug.	40,458	49,311	70,230	76,884
Sept.	29,174	41,159	65,410	74,964
Oct.	31,170	54,490	69,049	75,382
Nov.	43,174	51,553	61,029	73,411
Dec.	35,458	56,860	65,941	72,499
Totals	312,459	540,903	769,606	892,936
		+73%	+42%	+16%

	1990	1991	1992	1993
Jan.	72,441	77,171	92,703	100,682
Feb.	70,827	71,965	92,276	102,918
March	83,356	84,252	102,953	108,111
April	75,822	90,264	94,141	118,194
May	82,393	103,206	108,403	128,353
June	81,577	95,096	93,096	115,673
July	79,564	92,014	100,138	122,950
Aug.	81,115	97,533	111,988	117,795
Sept.	74,766	95,481	96,103	
Oct.	78,462	90,878	102,214	
Nov.	75,416	88,837	99,390	
Dec.	82,284	93,959	111,033	
Totals	938,023	1,080,656	1,204,438	
	+5%	+15%	+10%	

Miss Juan Pollo 1989 Lori Gonzalez

Miss Teen Juan Pollo 2002 Sharon Santoso

Miss Juan Pollo 2009 Desi Armstrong

Miss Juan Pollo 1995 - 2005 Jessica Hernandez

Miss Juan Pollo 2013 Michelle Davis
and TV hostess Chandra Brenner.

Miss Teen Juan Pollo 2002 Grace Lopez

Fourth of July Parade 1998 John Marshal, Jessica Hernandez & Zeke Soto Ontario, California.

Miss Juan Pollo 2011 Jessika Pulido and friends.

Custom made chicken costume 1985
designed by Martin Shiba-Noz

Official Juan Pollo mascot 2003   Chicken Costume from 1996

Chicken Costume from 1992

Miss Juan Pollo 2003 Angelica Carrasco   Miss Juan Pollo 2004 Priscilla Silveria

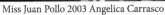

2011 Stephanie Twaite & Celeste Estrada

Miss Juan Pollo 2010 Lori Smalls   Miss Juan Pollo 2012 Malinda Ibarra

Juan Pollo Chicks support Pepsi-Cola bottling Riverside, Ca (2002)

Juan Pollo Chicks support West Coast Thunder Memorial Day Harley Run Riverside, Ca (2003)

KTLA Los Angeles Channel 5 Morning News Cinco de Mayo Celebration (2002)

KTLA Channel 5 Morning News Los Angeles Cinco de Mayo Celebration (2003)

Barstow, California Grand Opening Beauty Queen Miranda. (2005)

Sella cooking for new Ontario Grand Opening (2005)

Super Heros love Juan Pollo (2008)   Mr. and Mrs. Santa Claus visit Juan Pollo (2006)

Head cook preparing catering order, San Bernardino #2 Camillo Zamora (2012)

Cooking chicken the hard way. (2008)

Historic Site of the Original McDonald's museum. Free museum open daily 10am -5pm.
Mural depicting the History of San Bernardino painted by muralist Phil Yeh and friends.
Photo credit: AFreemanphotography.com

Desiah performing at 13th annual Veterans Day event hosted by Juan Pollo. (2012)

Juan Pollo corporate office and official Juan Pollo museum located inside Historic Site of the Original McDonald's museum. 1398 N E Street San Bernardino, Ca 92405

Black History Parade San Bernardino, California. (2012)

Young People Agree Juan Pollo Gets Thumb Up. (2012)

Actual Customer Comments 1988 - 1991

These pictures taken in the dining room and customers wrote their own uncensored comments. View these and more original Poloroids on display at Flagship location 1256 W. 5Th Street San Bernardino, California. (Over 600 Total)

Albert The Chicken Man
With A 50 Year Plan

Written Entirely By:

Albert R. Okura

Designed by:

LCM
®
PUBLISHING

The

more chicken I

sell, the fresher the

product... the fresher the product,

the better the quality... the better the quality,

the more people talk about us... the more people talk about us,

the more people find out about us... the more they find about us, the bigger

our customer base... the bigger our customer base, the more our sales... the

more our sales the fresher the product... the fresher the product.....etc...etc....

Legal pyramid scheme suggested by Albert in 1991